SQUEAKING
CLEOPATRAS

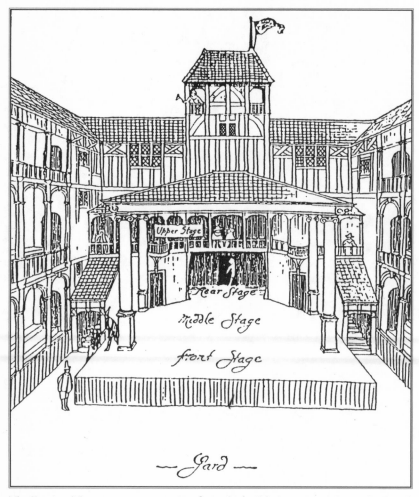

The Fortune Theatre: a reconstruction from the builder's contract. From the Royal National Theatre's programme for *Rosencrantz and Guildenstern are Dead*, 1995.

SQUEAKING CLEOPATRAS

The Elizabethan Boy Player

JOY LESLIE GIBSON

SUTTON PUBLISHING

To Alasdair Steven,
Julian Miller and Jonathan Burnett

'We have heard chimes at midnight'

First published in 2000 by
Sutton Publishing Limited · Phoenix Mill
Thrupp · Stroud · Gloucestershire · GL5 2BU

British Library Cataloguing in Publication Data
A catalogue record for this book is available from the British Library

ISBN 0-7509-2488-8

Typeset in 12/14pt Garamond
Typesetting and origination by
Sutton Publishing Limited
Printed and bound in England
by J.H. Haynes & Co. Ltd, Sparkford.

'. . . Our *Players* are not as the *players beyond sea, a sort of squirting baudie Comedians, that have whores and common curtizans to playe women's parts, and forbeare no immodest speech or unchaste action that may procure laughter, but our Sceane is more stately furnisht than ever it was in the time of* Roscius, *our representation honourable, and full of gallant resolution* . . .'

Gosson, Players connfuted in Five Actions (*1582*)

Contents

List of Illustrations

Frontispiece: The Fortune Theatre: a reconstruction from the builder's contract. From the Royal National Theatre's programme for *Rosencrantz and Guildenstern are Dead*, 1995.

Author's Note

Everyone who enjoys the plays of Shakespeare and his contemporaries has his or her own interpretation of the parts therein – this is one of the reasons why they still fascinate us today and why they are constantly being performed throughout the world. My interpretations are individual to myself and may not be those of my readers. Nonetheless, in exploring the women's roles to see whether they could be played by adolescent boys, though I have my own readings and ideas about the breathing patterns in the speeches, I found a consistency of writing that has made me bold enough to say that this is how it could have been. Nothing is certain when writing about the early modern period, all is interpreted, but if there are a number of instances of the same patterns occurring then it can be assumed, until further evidence is found, that the discoveries in this book are valid.

Acknowledgements

My gratitude to the Shakespeare Institute, within whose walls this book was researched and written, is immense and can never be repaid. I wish to thank especially Dr Russell Jackson for his encouragement and comments. The Director, Professor Peter Holland, allowed me to put aside other work to write this book, and James Shaw, the Librarian, was ever helpful. Dr Martin Wiggins enlightened me about the plays of Lyly and Marston in his usual erudite manner. Dr Susan Brock, the former librarian of the Institute, answered many queries.

The Librarians of the Shakespeare Centre and those of the Library of the Royal Borough of Kensington and Chelsea found books for me. The Deans and Archivists of the cathedrals mentioned in the text delved into archives and I have a special indebtedness to Dr Mayne of Westminster and Alice Oakley of Canterbury. Frances Cheetham and Brian Ayres of the Norwich Museum Service were informative about Elizabethan architecture, while the Warwick County Service also provided information. The staff of the Victoria & Albert Museum, Christie's Images, the Guildhall Library and the National Portrait Gallery provided illustrations. I have used interviews I conducted with actors when I was a journalist for which I thank them, especially Harriet Walter who was particularly illuminating.

Anyone who writes about the boys' companies owes a great and special debt to Professor Reavly Gair's book *The Children of St Paul's*, Michael Shapiro's *The Children of the Revels* and

E.K. Chambers' monumental work *The Elizabethan Stage*. Without these scholarly men we would know scarcely anything about these two important adjuncts to the Elizabethan theatre. Jane Crompton and Sarah Moore of Sutton Publishing have been delightful to work with. My thanks to them also, and all the other authors and scholars who helped and whom I consulted.

NOTE: All quotations from Shakespeare are taken from the *Compact Edition* of *The Complete Works*, published by Clarendon Press, 1991 edition. I have used the word Elizabethan throughout to designate the period between 1560 and 1642. The quotes that open each chapter are all from *Hamlet*. And the title is taken from Cleopatra's speech in *Antony and Cleopatra* Act 5 scene ii.

Introduction

'How like you the play?'

If, by some magic, we could travel in a spaceship and descend on Elizabethan England to go to the theatre, we would be astonished by one thing more than any other: the women's parts were played by boys. Indeed, in some theatres the entire cast was made up of boys, who were also choristers. This book is about those boys – the experiences they had, the skills they attained, how the playwrights helped them both technically and emotionally, how they were dressed and, finally, why the Elizabethans accepted this, to us, strange convention.

Although many books have been written about women's parts in Shakespeare's plays, treating the characters as though they were real women, no one, as far as I can ascertain, has considered the subject from the point of view of the boys themselves. Actresses find the parts fascinating and rewarding. As the actor Dame Edith Evans told writer Judith Cook:

> From the point of view of an actress, the Shakespearean women are most satisfactory people, for when portrayed they actually seem to feed the artist even when she is giving out the most of herself in the performance of her part. They are so true, their nobility, beauty, tenderness, loveliness, lightheartedness, subtlety, provocativeness, passion, vengefulness, worthlessness, stupidity and a hundred more qualities so entirely right from the feminine point of view that they provide a field the most ambitious artist could scarcely hope to recover.

However, Dame Edith would never play Lady Macbeth: she said that there was no explanation as to why the character went mad, and younger, perhaps better educated, actresses have said that they feel limited in their playing of Shakespeare's and his contemporaries' women's roles because the parts are underwritten. There are, of course, two points of view here. One that the characters are 'true', the other, that the actor has to 'fill in' the psychological processes of the character by imagination. Both approaches beg the question, could the boys have acted the parts satisfactorily?

It is the contention of this book that the boys were properly trained to act effectively and that the emotional content of the parts was well within the cognisance of a boy of the period, given the different experiences he would have had from a child of today and that the parts were written so he was not taxed technically nor physically.

I have assumed that boys would have been apprenticed around the age of ten as before that age a child would not have sufficient power of voice to be heard in an open-air theatre. The members of the boys' companies, some of whom were impressed at thirteen, played, as we shall see, in indoor theatres. Those apprenticed to the men's companies, progressed from walk-ons to small parts, probably around the age of thirteen, and would not have played main characters until they were seventeen or so, as discussed in Chapter Three. There is no evidence that the boys, unlike children at stage schools today, would have had any further education once they joined the company. Day by day, they would have been involved in productions, watching and observing, playing pages, fairies, anything they were told to. Today there is no real analogy to their experience, though boys in cathedral choir schools and the children of the Royal Ballet School, who work with professionals and who perform professionally, come near to it. By considering the training that boy choristers go through now, we can deduce the kind of apprenticeship boy players must have had, for the programme of professional education in choir schools is virtually the same today as it was in the sixteenth and seventeenth centuries. Indeed, the boy players had to sing and the breath control needed for this is more than valuable in making oneself heard in the theatre.

Are the emotions expressed by the women characters too complex and too deep for an adolescent boy to understand? This is another area examined in detail here and we discover that playwrights were skilful in limiting their emotional demands on the boys. It has often been observed that there are very few mothers in the plays and very little mothering. It is true that upper-class children saw very little of their parents at this time and mothering was not an attribute necessarily required, but the dramatists rarely write about those parts of a woman's life that are peculiar to her, such as motherhood, menstruation, pregnancy and childbirth. The Elizabethan woman was not expected to behave as the present-day woman does, and the attitudes to women are also part of this book.

What did the audiences actually see when they went to the theatre? All theatre is illusion and collusion and the prevalence of cross-dressing in Elizabethan society generally helped the boys to create an illusion of femininity. The vociferous protestations of the puritans about cross-dressing is to our unisex age amusing and diverting. The gorgeous clothes of the period with their ambiguity and splendour are illustrated in the many portraits and miniatures of the period and the spectacle on the Elizabethan stage must have been magnificent.

Shakespeare certainly writes about the widespread androgyny of his day, but not in any really salacious way. Where double meanings can be read into the text they are generally in character and somehow become more funny if said in a innocent way. Desdemona and Iago on the quayside indulge in witty, sexy talk but it is entirely in character: she is quite a bold lady and his sexuality has already been revealed. Helena in *All's Well that End's Well*, another independent woman who is a doctor's daughter, also speaks frankly, but again, this reveals her personality. Feminist critics often express the view that Shakespeare (and the other Elizabethan dramatists) 'degraded' women, taking *The Taming of the Shrew* and Posthumus's speech beginning 'It is a woman's part' as evidence. But this is to impute to Shakespeare the views his characters express. That he was aware of and could express the hatred that men can feel against women who have, or seem to have, been ill-behaved or unfaithful, is part of his ability as a great dramatist with an exceptional knowledge of human nature. To attempt to deduce Shakespeare's own views from the thoughts his characters express is a fruitless task. When Posthumus, Iago, Othello, Hamlet and Lear rail against the perfidy of women, they do not, in my opinion, in spite of their emotion, treat the women as sex-objects as some feminist critics have alleged. That they treat women differently by modern standards is obvious, but today we undervalue the traditional woman's role. And indeed, as we shall discover, women in Elizabeth's time had more complicated houses to run, with servants, apprentices and continual pregnancies. The tenet that women should behave and dress in a certain way is something that formed part of what a boy player was expected to do and something that, as we shall see, caused considerable discussion.

The boys were helped, too, by the way that the playwrights wrote for them. Chapters Four and Five are concerned with the mechanics of breath control. The reading of the parts must, of course, be individual but in studying all the texts of the women's parts in the works of Shakespeare and other principal Elizabethan and Jacobean writers, I discovered that no more than twenty-eight syllables, or two-and-a-half lines of iambic pentameter, need be spoken on one breath, a span which is well within the capacity of a trained, yet small-framed boy. It is not claimed that this span is unique to the boys' speeches – Shakespeare often used fragmented lines in the men's speeches to indicate heightened emotion – but for most of the men's characters longer phrasing is needed.

The other skills that the boys needed – gesture, dance and 'fencing – are also discussed and the emotional content of the parts is analysed, showing that boys were never expected to portray anything that was not within their emotional experience or anything that pertains to a woman's life and only to that life. The Elizabethan notion of femininity and dress was part of the knowledge that informed a boy's characterisation and the question of the prevalence of cross-dressing is something that will concern us.

Another fundamental difference the time-traveller would find between today's theatre and that of the sixteenth and seventeenth centuries would be the actual buildings. Though, especially since the reconstruction of Shakespeare's Globe Theatre in Southwark, London, the Swan in Stratford-upon-Avon, and the use of other spaces, this would come as less of a shock to us than previous generations who had experienced only proscenium arch theatres. John Stow's *Annales* lists the theatres in London in 1629:

> . . . there was builded a new faire Playhouse, neere the white Fryers. And this is the seventeenth Stage, or common Play-House, which hath bene new made within the space of three-score yeeres with London and the suburbs, viz. Five Innes, or common Osterues turned Play-Houses, one *Cockpit, S. Paules*, singing Schoole, one in *Black-fryers*, one in the *White-Fryers* which was built last of all . . . all the rest not named,

were erected only for common Playhouses, besides the new built Beare garden, which was built as well for playes, and Fencers prizes, as Bull Bayting; besides, one on former times at *Newington Butts*; Before the space of three-score years above sayd, I neither knew, heard, nor read, of any such Theaters, set Stages, or Play-houses as have been purposely built within mans memory.

As can be seen, not all the playing spaces were purpose-built and the Elizabethan actor, whatever his age, was used to performing in a variety of venues: the Great Hall of the Inns of Court; university colleges and noblemen's houses; and courtyards of hostelries (the New Inn at Gloucester is reputedly one) bull- and bear-baiting pits, which were all converted into spaces for plays. The players also travelled the length and breadth of England and Scotland, and overseas – there are records of English players touring Germany and Ireland at this time. There was even a performance of *Hamlet* on board a ship off the coast of Sierra Leone. But, of course, the main thrust of and impetus for this activity came from the theatres and dramatists in London. It was the theatres there that shaped the acting.

Shakespeare's company, the Lord Chamberlain's (later the King's Men) had two theatres, the Globe and the smaller indoor theatre, Blackfriars, which had previously been used by a boys' company. The other large, permanent company, the Admiral's Men, occupied the Rose. No measurements have been found for the Globe, but a specification remains for the Fortune Theatre, built in 1600, by Peyter Streete. In this document he is told to reproduce the same type of building that he had previously constructed – the Globe Theatre. The contract specifies some measurements for the Fortune and it is considered that the two theatres were virtually identical in size. As the contract states:

Thye frame of the saide howse to be sett square and to conteine
ffowerscore foot of lawfull assize every waie square without and fiftie
five foote of like assize square every waie within . . . And the saide
fframe to conteine three Stories in height, the first or lower storie to
containe Nyne foote of lawfull assize in heighth, the second Storie
Eleven foote of lawfull assize in heighth, and the third or upper Storie
to contaigne Nyne foote of lawfull assize in heighth . . . With a Stadge
and Tyreing howse to be made, erected and settup within the saide
frame, with a shadowe or cover over the saide Stadge, . . . and which
Stadge shall conteine in length Fortie and Three foote of lawfull assize
and in breadth to extend to the middle of the yarde of the saide howse;
the same Stadge to be paled in belowe with good, strong and
sufficyent new oken bourdes . . . And the saide Stadge to be in all
other proportions contrived and fashioned like unto the Stadge of the
saide Plaie howse called the Globe . . .

The playhouse was, then, 80 feet (24 metres) square on the
outside, and 55 feet (16.8 metres) on the inside. The stage itself
measured 43 feet (13 metres) across and thrust into the audience
by 26 feet 6 inches (8.4 metres). Recent interpretations of the
archaeological finds on the site in Southwark make the Globe
99 feet or 30 metres outside. They indicate it had twenty bays of
about 12 feet 6 inches deep joined to make a polygon of 270 feet of
running work.

A comparison with other spaces where plays are believed to have
been performed show that Middle Temple Hall measured 100 feet
(30.4 metres), including the entrance corridor behind the screen
and under the minstrel's screen at the east end, and 40 feet
(12.8 metres) across. The Boar's Head on the city boundary had a
yard of about 38 feet (12.2 metres) by 22 feet (7 metres). The
indoor theatre at Blackfriars, which James Burbage bought in
1596, was situated in the upper frater of a former monastery.

It measured 110 feet (33.5 metres) by 46 feet (14 metres) and the theatre contained therein was 66 feet (20.1 metres) north to south and 46 feet (14 metres) from east to west. It is not known whether the stage occupied the eastern end or whether it extended from the longer or south wall. In any case, it must have been smaller than the Globe, as in *The Doubtful Heir*, performed in 1640, James Shirley comments that the stage of the Globe was 'vast' compared to that of Blackfriars. The reconstituted Globe Theatre in Southwark, London, has an outer diameter of 100 feet (30 metres) and an inner diameter of 75 feet (22.5 metres). The stage is 46 feet (13.8 metres) wide, 22 feet 6 inches (7 metres) deep and 5 feet (1.5 metres) high. A present-day comparison as to size can be made with a double tennis court which is 80 feet (23.7 metres) by 36 feet 6 inches (10.9 metres), while a single tennis court is the same length but 30 feet (8.2 metres) wide.

At Stratford-upon-Avon, the Royal Shakespeare Company's Swan Theatre has a thrust stage which is 43 feet (13 metres) from the back wall to the front, where it is 19 feet 6 inches (5.9 metres) wide. The very size and shape of the Elizabethan stage, surrounded by an audience on three sides, influenced the texts of plays and led to a different style of acting from that used in a proscenium arch theatre nowadays, something our boy player would have to master. As actors in the new Swan have found, it is feasible to group players and to have them perform actions in a way that cannot work on a proscenium arch stage. An actor can address an audience in a more intimate way, making it possible for clowns to create a greater rapport, for example. This intimacy would also have made soliloquies more eloquent, for the actor could actually turn from one part of the audience to another thus bringing them into his or her inmost thoughts. John Barton, one of the RSC's greatest directors and exponents on speaking verse, thinks that there are very few rules to obey when speaking Shakespeare's lines but that a soliloquy must be shared with an audience. If an actor does this, then the soliloquy will really work. Toby Stephens, speaking of the difference between playing Coriolanus in the Swan and the Barbican Theatres, said that in the latter it was impossible to get the same degree of response from the audience as he had in the former. Both he and David Suchet say that at the Swan they are also conscious that most of the time some members of the audience could not see their faces. As Suchet wrote to the author, 'you must make sure that you don't stay in one position for too long because at any time someone is always going to see your back'. They both agreed that they had to make a particular effort to speak clearly and distinctly because of this.

At the back of the thrust stage would have been a tiring-house where the actors dressed and waited between entrances. This had a door at either side where the actors made their entrances and exits. Among the stage directions that show this is one from *3 Henry VI*, Act 2 scene v:

Alarum. Enter a son that hath killed his Father, at one door: and a Father that hath killed his Son at another.

Oberon and Titania in *A Midsummer Night's Dream*, Act 1 scene ii, also enter by separate doors, emphasising their differences even before their quarrel is mentioned in the text. Elizabethan stages almost certainly also had a door in the middle and, it is believed, that there was some inner recess at the back which could be curtained off, allowing a bed, table and chairs, or a throne to be set up for a succeeding scene. It could be used for hiding someone (Polonius in *Hamlet*) or discovering actors (Miranda and Ferdinand in *The Tempest* playing chess, for example). It would also have been a convenient place for someone to 'die'. Another feature of the stage was the trapdoor used for ghosts, apparitions and graves, and there was an acting area above the stage at the back. The stage was also partly covered by a canopy which was supported by pillars, and small pieces of scenery, such as bushes, benches or represent-ations of houses, could be moved off and on.

Costumes, as we shall see later, were sumptuous and in contemporary fashion, with period perhaps indicated by breast-plates, helmets, and togas. As the Sumptuary Laws decreed that only certain classes could wear certain fabrics or styles, the Elizabethans would instantly recognise a character's place in society or his profession by his dress.

So then, our boy player would be working on a large, bare stage with the minimum amount of scenery, which would have little visual appeal, and with absolutely no lighting effects. How then would he be able to convey to the audience the place or the time of day? The playwright always makes it quite clear where and when the action takes place:

Gallop apace you fiery-footed steeds (*Romeo and Juliet*: 3: ii)

. Are not these woods
More free than the envious courts? (*As You Like It*: 2: i)

What news on the Rialto? (*The Merchant of Venice*: 3: ii)

Though, once the location is firmly established the writer can change from lower to upper stage or to anywhere else that suits him. For example, in *Romeo and Juliet* the ballroom becomes the garden of the Capulets' house with Juliet's bedroom above: Romeo, after the wedding night climbs out of the bedroom window onto the stage, but then Juliet talks to her mother on that same stage in her bedroom, from which Romeo has just climbed. It is all done with words, not by change of scenery or lighting. The Elizabethans were made to use their imaginations far more than audiences today are accustomed to do.

So if we were sitting in the audience in 1600 at the first performance of *Hamlet* we would see a bare stage jutting into a surrounding audience who had paid a penny to stand, while above would be three tiers of seats costing more. On the platform would be gorgeously dressed actors moving so that their backs are not always towards the same part of the audience and including some part of the crowd in the dialogue at all times. They speak swiftly but distinctly in verse or prose that conveys complex thought and emotion. There is nothing much to distract the eye from them because there is little or no decoration on the stage and in outdoor theatres there is no lighting. All then is concentrated on the words and the story, for we have come to *hear* a play. The actors are within touching distance and the conditions make for intimacy and a sharing of an experience with friends. The very simplicity of the stage highlights the actors who convey not only the story and the emotions therein, but paint the scenery in words. Our biggest surprise on this day is that the two women's parts, Gertrude and Ophelia, are played by adolescent boys. What were these boys like? What were the experiences that enabled them to play these, and other parts, so well?

CHAPTER ONE

Education and Apprenticeships

'my two schoolfellows'

A child's life experience in the early modern period was totally
different from that of a child today. Indeed, by our standards
there was really no such thing as childhood; young people were
exposed almost from birth to all the unpleasant aspects of life.
Elizabethan houses for all but the prosperous were very small and
there was little privacy. The homes of the very poor have not
survived but those of the slightly better off – tradespeople, for
example – often consisted of one room downstairs and two above.
The corridor had not yet been adopted in construction, and
bedrooms, even of the very rich, led out of each other, the second
entered via the first. This lack of privacy throughout society meant
that life was lived in public, almost as if on stage. Even going to
the lavatory in large houses was an experience shared with other
people, as archaeological finds at Hampton Court have shown.
Sexual and bodily functions would be apparent to the observant
child; frequent pregnancies and childbirth without anaesthetics,
the cruelty of illnesses unrelieved by antibiotics and with only
herbal remedies to help, were there for all to see. Lack of basic
hygiene meant that Elizabethan and Jacobean men and women
would be exposed to all kinds of diseases that spread rapidly.
Influenza, the periodic, dreaded bubonic plague and the ever-

present smallpox attacked the population, resulting in many deaths. As John Donne, poet and priest, wrote in *Devotions*:

> Can the other world name so many venomouse, so many consuming, so many monstrous creatures as we can diseases of all these kinds? O beggarly riches.

Death, then, was constantly present in a way not generally experienced in Western society today. Men and women could marry several times in life after one or other party died young. Bess of Hardwick (*c.* 1526–1608) had four husbands, each richer than the last. Children themselves could have a limited lifespan, which made for an urgency in life – just as children who were in the Blitz in London during the Second World War learnt to cram in as much as possible in case they were killed in a raid, so the Elizabethans lived vividly.

The city of London grew from 250,000 people to 400,000 during Elizabeth's reign. Young people came to the capital to work in the growing financial profession, to the Inns of Court to be lawyers, to learn a trade, for London was fast becoming the commercial centre of Europe. They lived in crowded houses which were insanitary in the extreme. The streets were narrow and muddy, places where refuse would be thrown, where horses, coaches and carriages would all add to the dirt and confusion. It was a dangerous place to live: rogues, thieves, pickpockets and confidence men, called cony-catchers, were ready to swindle, especially the people just up from the country, as the plays of Ben Jonson describe all too well. One had to be hardy and streetwise to survive childhood and adolescence and even if one reached maturity there would probably be, at the most, twenty to thirty years more to live. An awareness of the frailty and fragility of life gives it an extra sharpness, something that would be an asset to an actor, who has to portray the immediacy of life on stage.

An added hazard to life was the extreme danger in which one could be placed by a cruel State. An implication in treasonable plots, criticism of the monarchy, dangerous friends, could all bring the wrath of the government against a person, resulting in prison, torture and a hideous death. Heads of traitors were exposed on London Bridge for all to see. Thomas Kyd, Ben Jonson, pamphleteers and printers all suffered under this harsh regime. And these events would have made an impression on the boys in the theatre. They might have witnessed one of the frequent public executions. It is estimated that 6,000 people were executed in the modern Greater London area during Elizabeth's reign, some for the most trivial offences; taking rises in population into account, this would be equivalent of 4,000 people a year now. Brandings, mutilations, whippings, being put in the stocks or pillory were events a boy could see daily. The cruel sports of bear- and bull-baiting and cock-fighting were well attended and some theatres were part-time with the bull pits. Taverns and brothels shared the South Bank of London with the theatres; the prostitutes leased houses from the Bishop of Winchester and were known as the Winchester Geese. Taverns were frequented by everyone, and could, for the unwary be hazardous places. Luke Hutton, hanged in 1598, describes (in *The Blacke Dogge of Newgate*, ?1598) an incident involving two women. Having attended the Accession Day tilts on the anniversary of Elizabeth's coronation, a brave spectacle when the gallants of Elizabeth's court dressed in armour and tilted against each other, they went to a tavern where they drank a pint of wine. When one of the women went to pay she found that her purse 'had been cut away'. As he walked to the theatre every day or sat in a tavern after a performance a boy would be aware of all this.

As an observant actor, for all actors have to be observant, he would stir these sights and sounds into his imagination and reproduce them on stage.

Yet there was also much to admire in London, including its public architecture. Fynes Moryson wrote in 1617:

> The Bridge of London is worthily to be numb'red among the miracles of the world, if men respect the building and foundation, laid artificially and stately over an ebbing and flowing water, upon twenty-one piles of stones, with twenty arches, under which barks may pass, the lowest foundation being (as they say) packs of wool, most durable against the force of water, and not to be repaired but upon a great fall of the waters, and by artificial turning or stopping the recourse of them. Or if men respect the houses built upon the bridge, as great and high as those of the firm land, so as a man cannot know that he passeth a bridge, but would judge himself to be in the street, save that the houses on both sides are combined in the top, making the passage somewhat dark, and that in some few open places the river Thames can be seen on both sides.

The river was the lifeblood of the city; barges came and went, bringing merchandise from all over the world to the wharves and jetties. It was a highway for aristocracy and ordinary folk alike. Indeed, a visit to the theatre was generally preceded by a row across it. Thomas Plater wrote in his diary (1599): 'On September 21st after lunch, about two o'clock, I and my party crossed the water, and there in the house with the thatched roof witnessed an excellent performance of the tragedy of the First Emperor Julius Caesar with a cast of some fifteen people.'

What of the people who came to the theatre, who were they and from what position in society did they come? Elizabethan society was hierarchical but the theatre attracted people from all its divisions. Andrew Gurr in his book *Playgoing in Shakespeare's London* has collected a list of names of people who are known to have gone to performances. They range from merchants to a 'junior gentleman', a butcher and a feltmaker, to Margaret Cavendish, Duchess of Norfolk, and ambassadors, as well as apprentices, students and sailors. The whole of the population is represented in Gurr's list. Throughout the literature, satires and ballads of the time there are references to playgoing. These, too, show the variety of people who attended a play. John Harrington describes a lady in an epigram:

A lady of great Birth, great reputation,
Clothed in seemly, and most sumptuous fashion
Wearing a border of rich Pearl and stone,
Esteemed at a hundred crowns alone,
To see a certaine interlude, repaires
To shun the press, by dark and privat staires.
Her page did beare a Torch that burnt but dimly.
Two cozening mates, seeing her deckt so trimly,
Did place themselves upon the stayres to watch her,
And thus they laid their plot to cunny-catch her:
One should as 'twere by chance strike out the light;
While th'other that should stand beneath her, might
Attempt (which modestie to suffer lothes)
Rudely to thrust his hands under her clothes
That while her handes repeld such grosse disorders
His mate might quickly slip away the borders.
Now though this act to her was most unpleasant
Yet being wise (as womens wits are present:)
Straight on her borders both her hands she cast,
And so with all her force she held them fast.
Villaines, she cryde, you would my borders have:

> But I'll save them, tother it selfe can save:
> Thus, while the Page had got more store of light,
> The cozening mates, for fear slipt out of sight.
> Thus her good wit, their cunning over-matcht,
> Were not these conycatchers conycatchd?

This epigram reveals the extremes of Elizabethan society all met at the theatre. The lady was going up the stairs to sit in one of the boxes for which she would have paid more than the penny admission that allowed people to stand – the groundlings. For sixpence one could sit on the side of the stage. Playwright Thomas Dekker writes disparagingly of this: '. . . what large comings-in are pursed up by sitting on the stage? First, a conspicuous eminence is gotten, by which means the best and essential parts of a gallant (good clothes, a proportionable leg, white hand, the Persian lock, and a tolerable beard) are perfectly revealed.' He goes on to list other ways in which for 'a good stool for sixpence' a young man can make himself noticeable and be the centre of attention.

Another epigram, this time by Sir John Davies, also shows the diversity of the audience:

> For as we see at all the play house dores,
> When ended is the play, the daunce, and song,
> A thousand townsemen, gentlemen, and whores,
> Porters and serving-men together throng . . .

As William Davenant showed in the Prologue of *The Unfortunate Lovers*, it was fashionable to visit the players in the tiring-house before the play started. Davenant writes:

. . . they to th'Theatre would come
Ere they had din'd to take up the best room;
Then sit on benches, not adorn'd with mats
And graciously did vail their high-crowned hats
To every half dress'd Player, as he still
Through th'hangings peep'd to see how th'house did fill.

Audience and players also mingled afterwards and, according to an apocryphal story, ladies made assignations with actors.

London audiences were not generally noted for their decorum and the atmosphere in theatres must have been quite lively. There are two references to theatres holding 3,000 people at a time, but doubt has been cast on this figure by the building of the new Globe, for there only 1,500 can be accommodated. Even allowing for modern fire regulations the discrepancy between the two figures seems rather large. Whatever the true attendance level, audiences made a significant impression. Stephen Gosson, in *The School of Abuse* (1579), wrote:

In our assemblies at plays in London, you shall see such heaving, and shoving, such itching and shouldering to sit by women: such care for their garments, that they be not trod on: such eyes to their lips, that no chips light in them, such pillows to their backs, that they take no hurt: such masking in their ears, I know not what: such giving them pippins to pass the time: such playing at foot-saunt without cards: such ticking, such toying, such smiling, such winking, and such manning them home, when the sports are ended, that it is a right comedy to mark their behaviour, to watch their conceits . . .

Another space in which actors performed was at the Inns of Court. The setting would approximate those of the playhouse,

Middle Temple Hall with its three doors and gallery being particularly suitable. Here the audience would be, if not more refined in their behaviour, more erudite in learning. It has been estimated that after leaving grammar school at fourteen, the average boy would be as proficient in Latin and Greek as a classics graduate today, so they would have been aware of and understood the classical allusions in plays.

The actors also appeared at the royal court: both Elizabeth and James enjoyed plays. Here, again, the actors came into contact with the aristocracy. Shakespeare's company, the King's Men, would wear James's livery. With the diverse venues at which they appeared, players were constantly mixing with both the highest and the lowest in the land.

What of a boy's life before he became an actor? The child might be motherless but he would in all probability be born into an extended family. If his father were a master-craftsman, and most boy players came from this stratum of society, there would be apprentices and journeymen in the household. There might be a maidservant, depending on how well his father was doing. He would certainly have shared a bedroom with his siblings and he would have been expected to do tasks either in the workshop or around the house as soon as he was able. He would probably have been beaten, for that was how children were punished. He would have worn skirts until he was seven years old, when he would have been breached and considered to be a responsible person. This would be an occasion for a ceremony, small in poor houses, of some grandeur among the aristocracy. There the boy would then be handed over to a governor and a tutor who would educate him at home with his brothers and sisters until the age of fourteen. The boys would go to university. The Elizabethan age was developing into a literate one, and textbooks were becoming increasingly available. Elizabeth's brother, Edward VI, founded many grammar schools and the tradition was carried on, prominent townsfolk often paying the master. At Stratford he received a good salary, £20 a year, so a boy living in town could have received a good education.

Although most schools were nominally free, there were certain expenses: pupils had to supply their own books, paper, candles and firewood. Some schools also had an entrance fee, or a small weekly levy. The boy player would certainly have been able to read, and read quite difficult poetry from cue sheets. He would, probably, have gone to a petty school at the age of four. Here children learnt to read. This would begin with reciting vowels and consonants, and some simple spelling. When they had mastered this, boys were taught the catechism by rote and then graduated to using a horn book. This was a wooden frame with a handle. Inside the frame would be a piece of parchment or paper on which was written the Our Father in English, as well as the alphabet. The whole would be covered in transparent horn. When the pupil could read this fluently he would be given the *ABC Book with the Catechism* from which he learnt the Ten Commandments and the Creed. The other book learnt from was the *Primer*. This contained psalms, litanies and parts of the Divine Office, for he would have been expected to be able to recite these correctly, especially if he wanted to go to grammar school. Religion was still central to life, and the other place where a boy would learn was at church. Attendance was mandatory and in addition to the service, it provided a central meeting place and a social occasion.

At school the child learnt to write, probably in secretary script, the most common form of writing, or the more fashionable italic script, which was becoming popular among the aristocracy. Elizabeth herself used the latter, while what writing we have of Shakespeare's indicates that he wrote the former. The keeping of simple accounts, or ciphering, was also taught.

After this, at the age of about six, the child began what is now called a humanist education. In the Elizabethan age classical literature and philosophy were widely appreciated and studied. Roman and Greek authors were quoted and admired and were considered models of good style. Correct or Ciceronian Latin became the paradigm and boys were expected to master its intricacies and elegances. Starting, as all Latin scholars have to, with declensions and conjugations mostly learnt by rote, the boy would soon be expected to be able to converse in Latin, and indeed would be penalised if he did not do so. Learning by rote also had the merit of teaching the children to speak clearly with good diction. In addition, it would help the boy to rely on his memory, thus training it so that he would be a quick 'study' when he came to learn parts. At eight, the potential boy player would leave the petty school and either go to a grammar school or take an apprenticeship. As William Harrison wrote in his *Description of England* in 1577: 'There are not many corporate towns under the Queen's dominion that hath not one grammar school at the least with a sufficient living for a master and usher.' Here the boy would continue his Latin and add Greek, and would be expected to speak one or the other all the time. The regulations of Canterbury School stated categorically in 1541 that 'Whatever they are doing, in earnest or in play, they must not speak any language but Latin or Greek.'

In rhetoric classes boys were also expected to speak English well. Richard Mulcaster, the Headmaster of the Merchant Taylors' School, in his book *Elementary* (1582) described English as 'a tongue of itself both deep in conceit and frank in delivery'. Mulcaster, and other masters followed his example, said that boys ought to act in Roman plays and to read poetry aloud. Children should be encouraged to master iambic verse, elegies and other verses and read them as loudly as possible with due attention to meaning and variety. A voice,

EDUCATION AND APPRENTICESHIPS

according to Mulcaster, 'should find in uttering how harsh and hard, how smooth and sweet it could be'. Mulcaster prized the English language and thought that children should be proficient in it for:

> While our religion was restrained to the Latin, it was either the only or the oneliest principle in learning, to learn to read Latin. But now that we are returned home to our English ABC, as most natural to our soil and most proper to our faith . . . we are to be directed by Nature and property [propriety] to read that first which we speak first, and to care for that most which we ever use most.

Another schoolmaster, John Brinsley, wrote in his book *Ludus Literarius* (1612) that masters should teach pupils: 'To pronounce every matter to the nature of it so much as you can: chiefly where persons or other things are feigned to speak . . . [he should] cause them to utter every dialogue lively as if they themselves were the persons which did speak in that dialogue . . .'

School days were long, eight or ten hours, and only Sundays, with obligatory church, were free. The day started at six in the morning in summer, an hour later in winter. There was a one- or two-hour break at eleven, then work started again until about five in the afternoon. Breakfast was at nine, dinner at eleven and supper would be taken (at home) at around seven at night. Discipline, by our standards, was exceptionally harsh, beatings being regularly given for any breach of decorum. One boy reported:

> I played my master a merry prank or play yesterday and therefore he hath taught me to sing a new song today. He hath made me to run a race (or course) that my buttocks doth sweat a bloody sweat. The more instantly that I prayed him to pardon me, the faster he laid upon. He hath taught me a lesson that I shall remember whilst I live.

My master hath beat my sides and back whiles the rod would hold his hand.

For an incipient boy player the most important subject of study would have been rhetoric – the art of speech and disputation. Thomas Heywood in his *An Apology for Actors* (1612) wrote that rhetoric:

> . . . not only emboldens a scholar to speak, but instructs him to speak well . . . to keep decorum in his countenance, neither to frown when he should smile, nor to make unseemly and disguised faces in the delivery of his words, not to stare with his eyes, draw awry his mouth, confound his voice in the hollow of his throat, or tear his words hastily betwixt his teeth. . . . It instructs him to fit his phrases to his action, and his action to his phrase, his pronunciation to them both . . . be his . . . pronunciation never so musical and plausive, yet without comely and eloquent gesture, a gracious and a bewitching kind of action . . . I hold the rest as nothing . . .

It is not known whether boy players went to grammar school. If they did, it is unlikely that they attended for longer than a year or so. There are no records of what ages boys joined a man's company, but it would not have been before the age of eight, the lowest age for becoming an apprentice. The members of boys' companies who joined the choir would have done so at the age of eight, then as now, as the records of cathedrals show. In *A Masque of Christmas*, Ben Jonson makes one of his characters, Venus, a deaf tire-woman, boast of her son who is playing the part of Cupid in some entertainment:

> Aye, forsooth, he'll say his part, I warrant him, as well as ere a Play boy of 'em all: I could ha' had money enough for him, and I would ha'

been tempted, an ha' let him out by the week to the King's Players. Master *Burbage* has been about and about with me; so has old *Mr Heminges* too; They ha' need of him . . .

From this we can infer that the players recruited talented boys wherever they found them and were sometimes prepared to pay the parents for the boy. This is also the subject of a speech in George Chapman's play *Mayday*:

Afore heaven 'tis a sweet-fac't child: methinks he would show well in woman's attire . . . I'll help thee to three crownes a week for him, and she can act well.

It is also possible that the men's companies would recruit boys who were or had performed with the boys' companies, particularly when these closed down, but as the boys were choristers they might not have been recruited until after their voices broke. The evidence for this is somewhat doubtful, though we do know that three Chapel Boys – Ostler, Field and Underwood – were both members of the Chapel Royal and acted with the King's Men.

Neither of Jonson's nor Chapman's words quoted above give any indication of the boys' ages. However, in his poem on the death of famous child actor Solomon Pavy, who appeared with the Children of St Paul's, Ben Jonson wrote:

Yeeres he numbered scarse thirteene
   When *Fates* turn'd cruell,
Yet three fill'd *Zodiackes* had he beene
   The stages jewell:
And did act (what now we mone)
   Old men so duely
As, sooth, the *Parcae* thought him one.

From this we learn that Pavy was ten when he first began to act. Nathan Field, another famous actor, and one who went on acting after his voice broke, was thirteen when he was 'pressed' into a boys' company.

The boy players in the men's companies would have been apprentices, one of the older actors acting as master. The actors had no guild: in order to have an apprentice, one had to be a master and to be a master one had to belong to a guild. But it was not obligatory to practise the trade of your guild – Ben Jonson, for example, belonged to the bricklayers', William Condell, son of Henry Condell, was a haberdasher, while the first Feste in *Twelfth Night*, Richard Armin, was a goldsmith's apprentice, his master being Iohn Louyson. John Lowin was also apprenticed to a goldsmith. John Heminges was a grocer and William Trigg, who was famous for playing women's parts, was apprenticed to Heminges. A master, whatever his trade, was responsible for training the boy to a great proficiency so that, after a period of being a journeyman, he could work on his own to produce whatever goods the master made. An apprenticeship could be entered into at any age. The Grocers' Company declared in an ordinance in 1595 that: '. . . no brother take an apprentice less than 8 or 9 years old or for less than eight years unless such apprentice be 21 years of age at least when he enters into his apprenticeship . . .'. But, as far as it is known, the players did not have such strict regulations, for the acting life of a boy depended on his voice remaining unbroken, an event that could not be foreseen. In the film *Shakespeare in Love* (1999) the fictional character Viola de Lesseps defies convention and appears as Juliet because the voice of the boy playing the part breaks before the opening performance.

Records of court cases show that boys were apprenticed for as long as twelve years or nine years and for as short a time as three years. In an agreement between one Martin Slater and the

Whitefriars Theatre (1609) it was agreed that all the children would be bound to Slater for three years. It seems that there was no set term. In his diary Philip Henslowe (d. *c*. 1616), builder of the Rose Theatre, manager and financier, mentions two boy players who were apprenticed to Thomas Dowton: 'Delivered unto Thomas Dowton's boy Thomas Parsons to buy divers things for the play of the Spencers the 16 of April 1599 the sum of £5.' The next year Thomas Dowton himself borrowed £2 to enable him to buy a costume for his boy in a play about Cupid and Psyche.

Other boys' names are culled from cast lists and include John Rice, who was apprenticed to John Heminges, while in his touching will (1605) Augustine Phillips, a leading member of the King's Men, left legacies to his apprentices Samuel Gilborne and James Sands:

> Item, I give to Samuel Gilborne, my late apprentice, the sum of forty shillings, and my mouse-coloured velvet hose, and a white taffeta doublet, a black taffeta suit, my purple cloak, sword, and dagger, and my base viol.

> Item, I give to James Sands, my apprentice, the sum of forty shillings, and a cittern, a bandore, and a lute to be paid and delivered unto him at the expiration of his term of years in his indenture.

Other valuable legacies to actors, particularly when they had to supply their own clothes and arms for the stage, were made to Robert Gough and John Edmans (generally assumed to have been Thomas Pope's apprentices), who were to divide Pope's apparel and arms between them.

The family of the boy to be apprenticed would generally pay a fee to the master, though, as has been seen from Ben Jonson's words, quoted above, the players would sometimes be prepared to pay parents to acquire a talented boy. Philip Henslowe, a theatre owner, noted in his diary that he 'Bought my boy James of William Augusten [an actor] the 18 of December 1597 for £8.' Henslowe also records that he received three shillings a week from the company for the boy.

William Prynne, who seemed to have hated everything to do with the theatre, railed against boys becoming players. Prynne (1600–69) was a puritan pamphleteer who wrote against the morals and manners of his age. In *Histrio-Matrix. The Players' Scourge* (1633), he said:

> Pity it is to consider how many ingenuous witty, comely youths, devoted to God in baptism, to whom they owe themselves, their services; are oft times by their graceless parents, even wholly consecrated to the Stage (the Devil's Chapel as the Fathers phrase it) where they are trained up in the School of Vice, the Play-house (as if their natures were not prone enough to sin, unless they had the help of art to back them) to vary excess of effeminacy, to act those womanish, whorish parts which Pagans would even blush to personate.

The boy would live with his master and would gradually be required to take part in the plays, firstly as walk-ons, pages, fairies, members of a crowd. There were no stage schools or drama schools for training – the boys would learn by watching and doing.

The relationship between the boys and their master's family could be an affectionate one as is shown by this letter from the apprentice John Pyk, dictated by him while his company was touring. Pyk writes to Mrs Alleyn:

> Mistress;
> Your honest, ancient, and loving servant Pig hath his humble commendation to you and to my good Master Henslowe and Mistress

and to my mistress' sister Bess for all her hard dealing with me I send her hearty commendations, hoping to be beholding to her again for the opening of the cupboard. And to my neighbor, Doll, for calling me up in the morning. . . . And though you all look for a ready return of my proper person yet I swear to you by the faith of a fustian king never to return till Fortune us bring with a joyful meeting to lovely London.

I cease, your petty, pretty, prattling, parling pig.

By me John Pyk

Mistress, I pray you keep this that my master may see it for I got one to write it, Mr Dowton, and my master knows not of it.

The letter was addressed:

To his loving Mistress Alleyn on the Bankside over against the Clink.

Of course, boys will always be boys, and doubtless they had to be disciplined. Some may have been sexually abused. But the Elizabethans did not recognise homosexuality, indeed the word did not exist. Living conditions meant that beds had to be shared, several people being in one, even at home. Sodomy was only punished by prosecution if it was carried out without the consent of the boy. It would be up to the master to be kind to his boys, for he would want them to work hard and be a credit to him, particularly if he had paid or was paying for him.

There is no record that the boy was paid wages. The shareholders, that is the senior actors of the company, such as Shakespeare, Burbage or Heminges took a part of the profits and the other actors were given wages. A master would, presumably, give a boy some pocket money and was responsible for his keep. The master's and the boys' fates were interdependent. Those who belonged to lesser actors (for then as now, the profession must have had those who were often out of work), the players who were called upon from time to time to take bit-parts, or who, through some fault of character, were not employed regularly, would have a rough time. When there was a plague outbreak all actors suffered. Those in the large companies could tour profitably, but the smaller companies would be out of work and the actors and boys could go hungry and have to sell their clothes and armoury, thus making it harder to get employment again. But boys could have a good time. A boy belonging to a leading player would have an interesting time, be well fed and clothed, work hard and prosper in his profession. They were probably fêted, praised and accepted by the aristocracy and gentry as guests. Indeed, Ben Jonson writes in *The Devil is an Ass* [2:iii]

Ingine:	Why, Sir your best will be one of the players!
Meercraft:	No, there's no trusting them. They'll talk on't,
	And tell their Poets.
Ingine:	What if they do? The jest
	Will brook the stage. But, there be some of 'em
	Are very honest lads. There's Dick Robinson,
	A very pretty fellow, and comes often
	To a gentleman's chamber, a friend of mine. We had
	The merriest supper of it there one night.
	The gentleman's landlady invited him to a Gossip's feast.
	Now he, sir, brought Dick Robinson,
	Dressed like a lawyer's wife amongst 'em all;
	(I lent him clothes) but to see him behave it,
	And lay the law, and carve, and drink unto 'em,
	And then talk bawdy, and send frolics! Oh!
	It would have burst your buttons, or not left you
	A seam.

Meercraft: They say he's an ingenious youth.
Ingine: Oh, sir! And dresses himself the best! Beyond
             Forty o' your very Ladies!

There is no contemporary English account of how the boy would spend his time, but a Spanish player, Agustin de Rojas has left a description of a Spanish actor's day:

> There is no Negro in Spain or slave in Algiers but has a better life than an actor. A slave works all day, but he sleeps at night; he has only one or two masters to please, but when he does what he is commanded, he fulfils his duty. But actors are up at dawn and write and study from five o'clock till nine, and from nine till twelve they are constantly rehearsing. They dine and then go to the comedia; leave the theatre at seven, and when they want rest they are called by the President of the Council, or the *alcades*, whom they must serve whenever it pleases them. I wonder how it is possible for them to study all their lives and be constantly on the road, for there is no labour that can equal theirs.

The boys, then, worked hard, depending on their master's benevolence, but a good master, as we have seen, gained the affection of his boy, for the boy could be a credit and a source of income for him. There must have been boys that were apprenticed and failed to have the requisite talent, for not all children can act, and while some seem to have a natural talent when young, that ability can fade or can cease with the loss of childish charm. Technique can carry an actor a long way, but technique alone cannot make an actor. The boys had to be well trained, they had to be encouraged and, above all, learn to act women naturally and well to an informed and critical audience.

CHAPTER TWO

To be a Woman

'your ladyship is nearer to heaven . . . by the altitude of a chopine'

Clothes were enormously important in Elizabethan England. In a society where status was a preoccupation, people showed who they were by what they wore. The Sumptuary Laws (Appendix Two) governed what an individual was allowed to wear and professionals, tradespeople and, above all, the aristocracy demonstrated their place in the social hierarchy by what they put on their back. In William Harrison's book *The Description of England* (1587) fashion is described thus:

> And these fashions are divers, so likewise it is a world to see the costliness and the curiosity, the excess and the vanity, the pomp and the bravery, the change and the variety, and finally the fickleness and the folly that is in all degrees, insomuch that nothing is so constant than inconstancy of attire.

Fynes Moryson (*Itinerary*, 1617) was caustic:

> They have in this one age worn out all the fashions of France and all the nations of Europe and tired their own inventions, which are no less busy in finding out new and ridiculous fashions than in scraping up money for such idle expenses.

The queen, herself, was always beautifully dressed, and her court was renowned for its magnificence. On visiting it, Brenning von

Buchenbach commented that: 'At no other Court have I seen so much splendour and fine clothes. This holds good both of the men and of the countesses and other noble ladies, who were of rare surpassing beauty.' And after Elizabeth, James's court was also renowned as one of the best-dressed in Europe, James spending far more on clothes than Elizabeth ever did. As accounts of the Wardrobe show, Elizabeth spent £9,535 in the last year of her reign, while James spent £36,377 annually. Elizabeth often had her clothes altered and relined if they were torn or soiled. As Janet Arnold writes:

> She dressed carefully for the part, but the story of Elizabeth's vast wardrobe turns out to be one of careful budgeting not of wild extravagance and vanity . . . the impression gained is that she regarded the rich silks . . . as state treasure; they were looked after most carefully. Some items dating from the 1560s were still there . . . in 1600.

At Hatfield House, Hertfordshire, there are two portraits of the queen which illustrate the magnificence of her clothes. One, the Ermine portrait, attributed to Nicholas Hilliard, shows the queen in a black dress decorated with jewels and gold rosettes (plate 5). A diadem is on her head, a gauze scarf round her shoulders, while the ruff and cuffs are of exquisite lace. In addition to diamonds, the queen is wearing ropes of pearls, and from these hangs the jewel known as the Three Brothers – three oblong diamonds set in a triangle round a pointed diamond and separated from each other by pearls. Another large pearl is suspended below. Her skirts are held out but not excessively so. The Iris portrait, attributed to Isaac Oliver, shows the queen as the goddess of the rainbow (plate 6). Here she is clad in a flowered dress and cloak with an orange lining. In her right hand is the rainbow and she is enveloped in a gauze cloak with a high wired collar; a second collar made of lace is attached to her dress. The edge is heavily embroidered with flowers. The queen also wears a very small ruff. On her left sleeve is a jewelled snake with a head like a celestial sphere from whose mouth hangs a red heart-shaped jewel. Pearls hang from one ear and all around the elaborate headdress. She wears a long, knotted rope of pearls and at her neck hangs another jewel.

Elizabeth's court was also extravagantly dressed, as the many portraits and miniatures show, and these were the standards of dress by which the players would be judged. The two Hatfield House portraits of the queen show the type of dress that would be worn in the theatre: the first for the part of a noblewoman, the second for a masque. Players had to provide their own clothes, the master being responsible for his boys, and often hired their costumes. Henslowe's diary, as we have seen, includes entries about clothes that were obtained for Dowton's boy. The players often bought their costumes from servants of the rich. When someone died it was customary for his clothes to be willed, as Phillips did to his boys. The servants, being prevented by law from wearing these sumptuous clothes, would sell them to players or to a broker (Henslowe was one). The brokers would hire out the clothes to the players or to people up in London from the country who wanted to dress more smartly.

Our boy player, then, if he were playing a noblewoman's part would be well dressed. He would have a lightly starched smock made of linen cambric or holland; it would have a drawstring neckline opening down the front and sleeves trimmed with lace which could hang down under the sleeves of the bodice. It would be either below the knee or ankle-length. This would also be worn in any scene requiring a nightgown. Stockings came next. Before the 1560s these would have been like gaiters made of wool, linen or silk and cut on the cross, buttoned up the sides. But in 1561, Alice

Montague, the queen's silkwoman presented her with a pair of knitted silk stockings and the queen declared she would never wear anything other. It is not known whether the boys wore these; they were certainly expensive. Perhaps, his master's wife might have knitted a boy some. Ben Jonson in the Prologue to *Bartholomew Fair* comments that an actor is delayed for his entrance because he is mending a fallen stitch in his stockings, which suggests the players did wear silk ones. They were made in fancy patterns. The stitch 'make-one', which produces lace-like effects, was much used, and the stockings could be embroidered and have 'clocks' or other decorations on them. They were held up by garters.

The most elaborate garment the boy would wear was a farthingale. This wide frame held out the petticoats and skirts, and came in a variety of shapes. Its most elaborate design, the drum, appears in a portrait of Elizabeth of Bohemia (plate 14). The frame was brought to England by Henry VIII's first wife Katherine of Aragon and the word comes from the Spanish *verdugado*, a corruption of smooth twigs, for supple twig-like pieces of wood were inserted into tucks of the underskirt. Some farthingales had rope instead of the wood. Katherine's was quite small and domed-shaped and it wasn't until Elizabeth's reign that it was extended to almost grotesque proportions. Round the waist was a bum-roll. It was a popular style as Meercraft in Ben Jonson's *The Devil is an Ass* says:

> An English widow who has lately travell'd,
> But she is called the Spaniard, cause she came
> Latest from hence and keeps the Spanish habit.

And when Margery in Thomas Dekker's *The Shoemaker's Holiday* itemises the clothes she is going to buy to match her new status she asks: 'Art though acquainted never a farthingale-maker, nor a

French-hood maker? I must enlarge my bum.' To make a farthingale would take around 5 yards of material and 7½ yards of rope. The Spanish was domed-shaped, while another style, the French was like an imported V. The *toiles* or patterns for these would have been imported from French tailors. The third style did not have any framework but was a loose-bodied gown like a university gown, but extended to the floor, open at the front and worn over a bodice and a slim skirt. John Webster refers to this style in *The Duchess of Malfi*.

In some styles the petticoats would be covered in an embroidered fabric while in others the topmost petticoat, or kirtle, would be made of some stiff and beautiful material in front – the part that showed – the back being of some more ordinary fabric such as linen. This might be plain, or if the character was high-born then it would be elaborately embroidered. Some French kirtles were pleated. The final skirt would be divided, again in an inverted V shape, edged with embroidered borders, to show off the skirt.

There were different styles of bodice, too. First there would be a stiffened underbodice. The most usual was like a man's doublet, what we today would call a jacket. Doing up at the front, sometimes with elaborate frogging but more usually with hooks and eyes, this would be high-necked and with sleeves that could either be long and plain or puffed, slashed and very elaborate, sometimes surmounted by pickadills, that is padded, crescent-shaped pads, or tied by busk-points (laces). The underbodice would also be embroidered. A ruff or lace collar would complete the jacket. Philip Stubbes in *The Anatomie of Abuses* (1583) fulminates against this fashion:

> The women there use great ruffs and neckkerchefs of Holland, lawn, cameric, and such cloth . . . then lest they should fall down, they are

smeared and starched in the Devil's liquor, I mean *Starch*; after that dried with great diligence, streaked, patted, and rubbed very nicely, and so applied to their goodly necks, and, withal, underpropped with supportasses . . . [they are] pleated and crested full curiously . . . Then last of all, they are . . . clogged with gold, silver or silk lace of stately price.

Another neck style was the rebato which was a wired gauze collar which stood up at the back of the neck.

Then came a partlet. This was a decorative yoke that covered the throat to the edge of the bodice and could be made of linen, damask or net. For court, the women wore elongated, boned bodices which ended in a point stiffened with buckram. Often this had an inset, heavily jewelled, and it was very low cut. A ruff or a rebato finished this style.

In the 1590s it was the fashion to wear gauze aprons of which the poet George Gosson wrote:

These aprons white of finest thread
So choicely tied, so dearly bought
So finely fringed, so nicely spread
So quaintly cut, so richly wrought.

Over this, outdoors, women wore cloaks. Shoes, made of Spanish or English leather, sometimes in velvet, were pinked and slashed, and until 1590 heelless. They had high fronts, somewhat like a loafer today, and could be decorated with jewels and rosettes. The soles were of cork. Stubbes describes them:

. . . whereto they have corked shoes, pinsets, pantofles, and slippers, some of black velvet . . . white, green, and yellow; some of Spanish leather and some of English, stitched with silk and embroidered with gold and silver all over the foot, with other gewgaws innumerable.

For walking through slush of London or muddy country paths, a chopine was put on. These were little wooden stilts which would not only protect the shoes but keep skirts out of the filth and mud. For court, elaborate headdresses would be worn, for going out a bonnet or coptain hat (see Chapter Nine). Other accessories would include fine linen handkerchiefs, often embroidered like Desdemona's, and fans, which the boys would have to learn to manipulate. Stubbes enumerates other accessories:

> Their fingers must be decked with gold, silver and precious stones, their wrists with bracelets and armlets of gold and other costly jewels, their hands covered with their sweet washed gloves embroidered with gold, silver, and what not; and to such abomination is it grown as they must have their looking glasses carried with them wheresoever they go. . . . Then they must have their silk scarves cast about their faces and fluttering in the wind, with great tassels at every end either of gold, silver or silk. . . . When they ride abroad they have visors made of velvet . . . wherewith they cover all their faces, having holes made in them against their eyes, whereout they look.

The fabrics were gorgeous: grosgrain, damasks, taffetas, satins, sarcenets, velvet and three-pile velvet. In the latter, the loops of the velvet were cut by hand into three different lengths to create a pattern in depth. The fabrics were, according to Stubbes, very costly: 'ten, twenty, forty shillings a yard'. The bill for materials for one masque given in honour of the queen came to £32, this at a time when £5 was considered a good yearly wage.

Undergarments were linen or lawn, a very fine linen. Fine wools might also be worn in winter, the queen sometimes wearing stockings of fine worsted. Colours, too, were luscious. Though black was a favourite, rich reds, such as carnation, scarlet and crimson, were often chosen. The queen liked her ladies-in-waiting to wear white, black, gold or silver to form a background to her more flamboyant clothes, which were selected to complement her own red and ivory colouring – russets, black, white, ash and gold were favoured and all can be found in her portraits.

London citizens' wives were limited in the materials they could wear, but so rich were they becoming that the Sumptuary Laws were often disobeyed and visitors to the capital were surprised at the luxury displayed. Even if the citizens did not wear the silks and satins of the court, they wore beautiful worsted wools and a fabric called linsey-wolsey, which was a mixture of wool and linen. The lines of the farthingale were more restricted outside the court; one needed plenty of space when wearing one and the limited room in ordinary houses probably meant that a small bum-roll and petticoats sufficed for most women. A small ruff or lace collar might be worn, but a kerchief was usual for everyday. The apron would be of holland when doing domestic chores, of gauze for later in the day or when receiving guests. That some women could afford beautifully embroidered clothes even of the merchant class is indicated by plates 9 and 10. In 1994 the Victoria and Albert Museum acquired a doublet made for Margaret Laton, the daughter of a rich London grocer and the wife of Francis Laton, a Yorkshireman who became the Master of the Royal Jewels. It has been speculated that the garment could have been made in the Royal Wardrobe and dates from about 1610. The doublet is in cream silk, lined in carnation silk. Embroidered with flowers, butterflies and snails, it is trimmed with gold lace on the turned-back cuffs, round the neck and down the front. What makes this doublet interesting, besides its survival over four centuries, is that it is accompanied by a portrait of Margaret. In it she is wearing a lace bonnet, trimmed with red feathers. A deep lace ruff encases her throat and her shoulders are covered with a black lace shawl. Deep lace cuffs are, presumably, tucked into the doublet's own cuffs, while a gauze apron with an embroidered belt masks a red skirt. The skirt is quite narrow and seems not to be supported by either a bum-roll or a farthingale: either the skirt or the apron is embroidered. It is altogether a beautiful and sumptuous outfit which shows how luxurious even merchants wives' clothes could be.

Lower down the social scale materials and clothes would be more simple, similar to the citizen's wife in plate 4 with her coptain hat, kerchief and narrow skirts. When Innogen in *Cymbeline* decides to go to Milford Haven to see Posthumus, she first of all wears a costume fitting for a franklin's wife which would have been similar to this illustration. There were riding habits, too. Women rode side-saddle. They would wear a saveguard (a full and gathered overskirt), which could have been worn over breeches, or the more fashionable might just have worn breeches.

Headdresses and wigs were worn, the rich sporting jewelled ones. In Mary Tudor's reign (1553–8) the French hood was a favoured headdress, and the National Portrait Gallery has a painting of her wearing it. A stiffened bonnet in front, it has a tubular velvet snood behind. By the 1590s this was no longer *de rigueur* among the aristocracy, but citizens' wives still aspired to wearing one and there are references to it in the plays. The use of make-up, naturally brought down upon its wearers the fury of the puritan pamphleteers, Philip Stubbes being particularly irate:

> The women of Ailgna [England] use to colour their faces with certain oils, liquors, ungents and waters made to that end, whereby they think their beauty is greatly decored.

And of hair he continues:

> If curling and laying out their own natural hair were all . . . but they
> are not simply content with their own hair, but they buy other hair,
> dying it of what colour they list themselves. . . . Then on top of these
> stately turrets . . . stand other capital ornaments, as the French hood,
> hat, cap, kercher and such like whereof some be of velvet, some of
> taffety, some (but few) of wool.

Ben Jonson has fun with the susceptibility to cosmetics and
fashion in *Epicene*.

Sometimes, of course, the boy player donned male attire. If he
were playing a page or a serving-man he would wear a livery. The
royal livery was scarlet and a special tailor in the queen's wardrobe
was employed to make it. In James's reign, Shakespeare's company
would have worn it at court or in any procession in which it was
asked to take part. The livery coat took 3 yards of material and
2 yards of velvet to garde (that is trim) it. Ordinary liveries were
generally of blue material, though russet, grey and tawny were also
used, and provided by the man or woman the page served, as part
of the servants' wages. There were summer and winter liveries and
each would have the badge with the cognisance of the household
embroidered on the left sleeve. As a charming scene in *The Merry
Wives of Windsor* shows, it was a treat for a page to be given a new
livery.

If, like Viola, the character was of good standing, then the
costume would have been lavish, and as complicated as that of any
woman. The colours would be rich and dark, black being a
favourite colour. But the darkness would have been relieved by
embroidery, or slashing, where differently coloured lining was
pulled through holes in the outer garment. Courtiers wore more

flamboyant colours and more extreme styles. The doublet, worn over a fine shirt or smock, trimmed with embroidery and lace, was the main upper garment. Like the women's it was padded and embroidered, curved to a point over or below the waist. As the sixteenth century progressed so the doublet became more exaggerated and ballooned out to give a pouter-pigeon shape. Later, there was a fashion for the doublet to be worn loose and undone with a soft lace collar falling over the edge. Over the doublet in cold weather would be a jerkin. This was loose and mostly sleeveless, the large sleeves of the doublet precluding any over-sleeves.

Round the waist would be a leather, tooled belt with carriers for a rapier and dagger, the mark of a gentleman. The doublet was joined to the upper hose by threading points, or laces, through eyelet holes round the waistline of both garments, hose being not stockings, but breeches. These also came in a variety of styles. The fashionable would wear round, puffed-up, slashed breeches which were pulled up high on the thigh. These were known as Spanish kettledrums. Ribbons, called panes, were superimposed on the top of the main fabric, which created a striped effect. There were also galliskins, which were longer, and slops, which came below the knee. These are the type of breeches seen in the frontispiece of *The Roaring Girl*, which might also be one of the few representations of a boy player that we have (plate 13).

On the legs would be the nether hose, or netherstockings, which might be, like the women's, made of fabric cut on the cross, or, increasingly, knitted ones. These could also be joined to the breeches by points, or held up by garters. The whole costume would be finished by a wide ruff or deep lace collar. Cloaks were worn out of doors, hats and gloves completed the outfit. Shoes came in a variety of types – indoors a pump similar to those worn by women, slashed and embroidered, while out of doors either an ankle boot or, for riding, a boot to the calf or knee. Pantofles were worn as overshoes to protect the smarter, more delicate pumps from the mud. The other garment used by men was the gown, which the academic gown today resembles. It was worn mainly by elderly men in public or at home, as men today might wear a dressing-gown to relax in.

Rosalind in *As You Like It* refers to her doublet and hose. How elaborate this was is hard to tell. Probably he/she did wear these garments, but of a more simple nature than those worn by gentlemen, more akin to those worn by Moll in *The Roaring Girl*. In the *Merchant of Venice* Portia and her maid Nerissa would wear a lawyer's gown and cap, Jessica something paltry, as her father Shylock was careful with money. Julia's disguise is described in the text (see Chapter Nine). Innogen's and Viola's would be elaborate and Viola's was a copy of her brother's.

In addition to dressing like a woman the boy player had to assume her qualities. The dress would have helped. RSC actor Ken Saberton, in his first job after leaving drama school, played Celia in *As You Like It*. In the first scene his dress had a train and 'that really taught me how to walk like a woman'. The boy also had to learn to curtsy, manage a fan, and wear a wig and make-up. There was more. What the boys had to convey not only with costume but also by voice, gesture and imagination was a truthful portrayal of a woman of that period, a Renaissance woman. The boys had words given to them, but it was up to them to fill out the part and make it real. What, then, were these ideals of womanhood to which they had to aspire?

A woman had to be circumspect. From the Middle Ages onwards there had been the so-called courtesy books and sermons preached from pulpits to remind women that theirs was the fault which had caused man's fall in the Garden of Eden. God had put man to rule women and she had to obey, for her father and later her husband had authority over her. From the book written for his young wife by the Menagerie de Paris to Castiglione's *The Book of the Courtier* and beyond, women were entreated to be good housewives, look after their men, their households and the children and, above all, to behave modestly. The Menagerie tells his fifteen-year-old wife that, among other things, it is her duty to 'keep him in clean linen, for that is your business'. She had a large household to look after, and besides the linen, she had to attend to the cooking, the brewing and be a nurse to nearly a hundred people. The Menagerie was a rich merchant and, doubtless, the routine of his household in Paris was duplicated in rich merchants' houses in London. Lower down the social scale there would be houses with just a handful of servants and one or two apprentices, all of whose welfare depended on the efficient housewife. Castiglione's *The Book of the Courtier* had great influence over the Elizabethans, the first English translation by Sir Thomas Hoby being published in 1561. *The Governor* (1538), by Sir Thomas Elyiot, and Roger Ascham's *The Schoolmaster*, published posthumously in 1570, laid down the principles of good behaviour for both men and women, and imitated or recommended Castiglione's work. The latter's influence on Sir Philip Sidney, Ben Jonson and William Shakespeare is apparent in their work. Castiglione was quite explicit in his ideas on both gesture and behaviour where women were concerned. He advocated an 'uncontrived simplicity' and 'simple and natural gestures'. He thought that women should not be heavily made-up, for:

> Surely you realize how much more graceful a woman is who, if indeed she wishes to do so, paints herself so sparingly and so little that whoever looks at her is unsure whether she is made-up or not, in

comparison with one whose face is so encrusted that she seems to be wearing a mask and who dare not laugh for fear of causing it to crack.

He liked artlessness, too, in displaying good features such as lovely teeth or beautiful hands (these could languish over a farthingale as we see in several of Elizabeth's portraits). Everything should be done skilfully and sparingly, not obviously, so that a desire to see more would be encouraged. And Castiglione says:

> Surely, too, you have sometime noticed when a woman, passing along the street on her way perhaps to church, happens in play or for some other reason, to raise just enough of her skirts to reveal her foot and often a little of her leg as well. Does it not strike you as a truly graceful sight if she is seen just at that moment, delightfully feminine, showing velvet ribbons and pretty stockings?

If a boy player read or was told this, he could seize on the gesture for Beatrice-Joanna in the first scene of *The Changeling* by Thomas Middleton (1622). Castiglione goes on to praise behaviour in which '. . . affectation is avoided or hidden; and now you can see how incompatible it is with gracefulness and how it robs of charm every movement of the body or of the soul'.

Later, Castiglione differentiates between the behaviour of men and women:

> . . . for although they have in common some qualities, which are necessary to the man as to the woman, there are yet others again befitting a woman rather than a man, and others again which befit a man but which a woman should regard as completely foreign to her . . . but, above all, I hold that a woman should in no way resemble a man as regards her ways, her manners, words, gestures and bearing. Thus just as it is fitting that a man should display a certain robust and sturdy

manliness, so it is well for a woman to have a certain soft and delicate tenderness, with an air of feminine sweetness in her every movement, which, in her going or staying and whatsoever she does, always makes her appear a woman.

A good woman has to:

> . . . shun affectation: to be naturally graceful: to be well-mannered, clever and prudent: to be neither proud, envious or evil-tongued, nor vain, contentious or clumsy. . . . She must also be more circumspect and at greater pains to avoid giving an excuse for someone to speak ill of her; she should not only be beyond reproach but also beyond even suspicion, for a woman lacks a man's resources when it comes to defending herself.

This, then, was the pattern of gentle womanhood that a boy player had to emulate. It is, of course, similar to the one that Katherine pronounces in the last act of *The Taming of the Shrew*. Women should speak quietly (though loud enough to be heard on the stage) – a too pert woman was deprecated. As King Lear puts it:

> Her voice was ever soft
> Gentle and low, an excellent thing in woman. (Act 3:v)

Beatrice in *Much Ado About Nothing* is reproved for her caustic speech, Benedick exclaiming:

> O God, sir, here's a dish I love not. I cannot endure my Lady Tongue.

And Katherine was called 'Kate the cursed' because of her bad behaviour, while Coriolanus praises his wife as 'My gracious silence'.

Not only were women expected to behave with decorum, they were also required to be obedient, first to their fathers and then, upon marriage, to their husbands. So the ideal woman was graceful, quiet and decorative, qualities which a boy would be expected to portray. To be subservient to men would be something that he would be quite used to: he would, at all times, have to be obedient not only to his master but also to the other shareholders in the company and the playwright. Many of the heroines, though, don male attire and a boy actor would be able to have great fun and show his skills by juxtaposing male and female behaviour, portraying the delight of the female as she assumes more assertive behaviour. The double standard of behaviour forms part of the comedy of many of the plays, including *As You Like It*, *Twelfth Night* and *The Roaring Girl*.

Women, though, have a physical life which is entirely different from that of a man and something no male could ever truly comprehend, however empathetic he was towards it. The events of her life that make a woman peculiarly a woman are menstruation, pregnancy, miscarriage and childbirth. How do the playwrights of the early modern period deal with these? The answer is mainly by ignoring them or by touching on them only lightly. Menstruation is never discussed: Shakespeare makes one reference to it in *The Tempest* but the words are spoken by a man and as a metaphor, nothing is ever said about how a woman feels at this time, nor do girls get together to discuss it as they do in real life. But this is common to all literature (except pornography and the Bible) up until the present day. Even now, it is not a subject that has been dealt with in the theatre.

There are pregnant woman in the plays – Helena in *All's Well That Ends Well* has to achieve pregnancy before Bertram will acknowledge her as his wife and, by means of the bed trick, she does. This is treated as comedy, and there is no mention of the inconveniences of the state nor is the pregnancy carried to full term – it is just the solution to Helena's dilemma.

Julietta is pregnant in *Measure for Measure* but this is a plot device and is, again, not explored. A more dramatic use of pregnancy comes in *The Duchess of Malfi* by John Webster where Bosola suspects that the Duchess is pregnant by her steward Antonio but needs proof. She is wearing a loose-bodiced gown which may be disguising it. He sets a trap for her:

> *Bosola*:   I have a present for your Grace.
> *Duchess*:   For me, sir?
> *Bosola*:   Apricocks, Madam.
> *Duchess*:   O sir, where are they?
>   I have heard of none to-year.
> *Bosola*:   (aside) Good, her colour rises.

The Duchess eats the apricots greedily and discusses them while Bosola muses:

> *Bosola*:   How greedily she eats them!
>   A whirlwind strike off these bawd farthingales,
>   For, but for that, and the loose bodied gown,
>   I should have discover'd apparently
>   The young springal cutting a caper in her belly.

The Duchess becomes ill and Bosola's suspicions are proved. There is no discussion of her condition and she goes on to have at least one other child without any details being given. Hermione in *The Winter's Tale* is also with child but, again, except for a little weariness, does not seem to suffer from her condition. She has to stand trial very soon after the birth. She has to stand trial very soon after the birth of Perdita, and Perdita's birth, like Marina's in *Pericles*, takes place offstage. Jacquenetta in *Love's Labours Lost* is only two months pregnant and Julietta in *Measure for Measure*, a few months. Few characters show any of the soreness or weakness of the aftermath of birth, so a boy player would not necessarily have to portray this, though probably having witnessed births in his own environment he would be fully aware of what was involved. It is rare to see such events on the stage even today though not on television, which depicts pregnancy, miscarriage and childbirth in graphic detail. The Elizabethan dramatists may have been reluctant to write about these subjects, not having had any first-hand experience of them.

Childbirth leads to motherhood, and this might be difficult for a boy to act. He would, of course, have a mother-figure in his life – his own mother, a step-mother or his master's wife. Elizabethan children did not, though, experience the affection that children with good parents do today. Royal children had their own households from a very early age, with their own servants as befitted their rank, the household being run by a governor or governess. The aristocracy sent their sons and daughters to houses where they could make a suitable match, while citizens' children, or children of poorer parents, were often sent away for their apprenticeships. Mothering was not a quality that was much appreciated and this is reflected in the plays, for very few mothers appear. It could be argued that the reason for this is because boys were playing women's parts. We do not see the Duchess of Malfi with her children, though she has an affecting speech about them before she dies. Hermione and Lady MacDuff do have charming scenes with their children, but they are very short, and show nothing of the difficult relationships that mothers and children can

1. Elizabeth Cecil, Mistress Wentworth, or Elizabeth Brook, Lady Cecil. This is the type of costume that a boy player would wear when taking the role of an aristocrat.

2. The Swan Theatre, Stratford-upon-Avon. A modern interpretation of an Elizabethan theatre.

3. A schoolroom, woodcut from Alexander Nowell, *Catechismus parvus pueris primum qui ediscatur, proponendus in Scholis* (1574 edition).

Marchants wife of London

W Hollar fec

Ciuis Londinensis melioris qualitatis Vxor.

2

4. A merchant's wife, *c.* 1630, by Wenceslas Hollar. A dress like this would have been worn by the boys in a citizen comedy.

5. Queen Elizabeth, the Ermine portrait.

6. Queen Elizabeth, the Iris or Rainbow portrait.

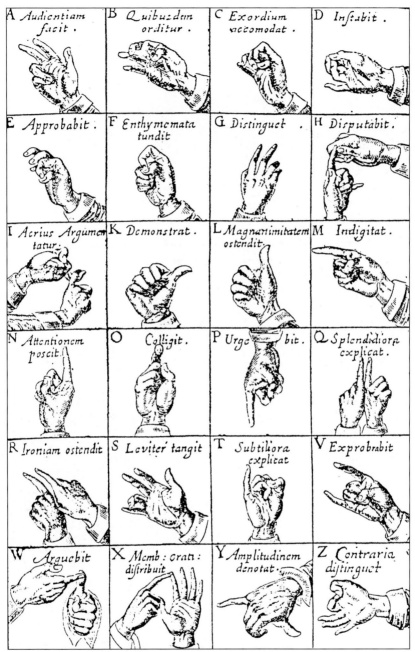

7. Gestures from John Bulwer's *Chirologia or the Naturall Language of the Hand* (1644).

8. *The Booke of Faulconrie* (1575), which shows how elaborate men's clothes were. The boy player would have worn something like this when 'she' was disguised.

9. A jacket worn by Margaret Laton, *c.* 1615, which shows how luxurious even merchants wives' clothes could be.

10. Margaret Laton wearing the jacket in plate 9.

11. Frontispiece to the 1630 Quarto of *Arden of Faversham* showing the murder scene.

12. A contemporary woodcut used as a title page to the 1615 edition of *The Spanish Tragedy* by Thomas Kyd (1587).

have. Elizabeth Woodville has a scene mourning her sons in
Richard III and her younger son has a pert scene, earlier in the play,
with his grandmother, but these pieces are not specifically about
motherhood. There are no scenes where a child is petted, played
with, taught to read, though one does occur in *The Merry Wives of
Windsor* where a son is made to show off his learning to his
ignorant mother. There are no babies teething, being sick or
wanting their nappies changed. It is significant that in the plays of
Shakespeare, though there are a number of fathers with daughters
there are hardly any mothers of girls. Thais and Hermione only
meet Marina and Perdita at the end of the plays *Pericles* and *The
Winter's Tale* respectively. Juliet is shown with her mother but that
relationship is hardly a good one, being very formal and rather
harsh. Juliet does have a surrogate mother in the Nurse, but as the
play progresses she treats the older woman more and more like a
servant, giving her orders in a way that no girl of that time would
have been allowed to give her mother. A boy would more easily
relate to a mother–son relationship than a mother–daughter one,
so the absence of mothers with daughters would help the boy
players.

There are two mothers of sons who do play a prominent part in
their respective plays – Gertrude and Volumnia. In the scenes
between Hamlet and his mother, Gertrude is the victim of his
vituperation and scorn and as she is not the instigator, the impetus
of the scene being with him, she simply has to react with distress,
an emotion known to every child. Volumnia is a dominant mother
– bold, outspoken, opinionated and ambitious for her son. These
are qualities that any actor would relish, and those which the
modern-day stage mother has, and doubtless there were stage
mothers in Shakespeare's day too! This is a part of strong emotions,
which are easier to act than gentle, docile ones.

One of the most important things to happen to a woman is falling in love. Indeed, a later poet declared it to be 'woman's whole existence' and there is a lot of falling in love in the romantic comedies and tragedies too. But is it love as experienced in real life? Nowadays, in literature and on television love, or sex, is very explicit. The Elizabethan playwrights, even if the conventions of the time allowed it, could not show naked boys in love scenes, for it would have immediately destroyed the illusion that they were women. Falling in love is not only an adult emotion; children fall in love, have crushes and idolise someone with longing. Even if a particular boy player had never fallen in love he would have observed the phenomenon and could read about it. Elizabethan love poetry is among the most erotic.

The three strands that influence both the age's poetry and its attitude to love come from the French troubador tradition, from the Italian sonnet and from the then newly discovered *Symposium* of Plato. Each of these has a distinct aspect. The troubador songs were long familiar in England as a result of the Angevin Empire in the twelfth century. Henry II's queen, Eleanor, set up a Court of Troubadors in her dukedom of Aquitaine, and her third son, the Coeur de Lion, was himself a troubador. The songs of the troubadors were in two veins – the courtly, where the lady was worshipped but not touched, and the erotic, which dealt in a pleasant strain of bawdy:

> Her lover takes her in his arms
> And in a great bed they lie alone;
> Fair Yoland straight does kiss him then
> As freely in half the bed they lie!
> God, how sweet is the name of love!
> I never thought to feel its pain.

Or:

> When my wooing brought me naught
> On the ground I laid her straight
> Lifted up her pretty dress
> And seeing her white nakedness
> Burned all the more
> And taught her love's lore;
> Nor did she say me nay
> But delighted in the play.

Or more violently:

> When my plea has brought me naught
> By the waist I seize her, by her shining fleash,
> Lift up her skirt
> And her white petticoat.

The Italian sonnet form, used extensively by Wyatt, Sidney and Spenser, had a more stately and courtly feel. Sidney's *Astrophel and Stella* has scenes in it that are full of passion, but it is passionate not sexually explicit and not overt. Plato's *Symposium* is a discussion on love in which the highest form is considered to be spiritual passion between two men. This is considered higher than the love of men for women, which is pleasurable, and necessary for procreation. Altogether, these influences formed an Elizabethan idea of love which was totally different from the ones we have of love today. There was a fluidity about sexuality in Elizabethan times, as Shakespeare's *Sonnets* show if we consider them as being written from experience, for they tell of a man who could love both a dark lady and also someone who was 'the master-mistress of his passion'. The terms homosexual, bisexual and heterosexual are not Elizabethan but the invention of a more prurient age.

Taking inspiration from love John Donne could write:

License my roving hands, and let them go,
Before, behind, between, above, below.
O my America! My new-found land,
My kingdom, safeliest when with one man man'd.

Christopher Marlowe could describe love also:

And oftentimes into her bosom flew,
And about her naked neck his bare arms threw,
And laid his childish head upon her breast,
And with still panting rock'd there took his rest.

And:

Even as delicious meat is to the taste
So was his neck in touching, and surpass'd
The white of Pelop's shoulder. I could tell ye
How smooth his breast was.

There is no evidence that the boys read this poetry, but particularly as Shakespeare and Marlowe were playwrights they might have heard the works discussed, quoted and spoken. It was an introduction of the feelings of love that could, and must, have stimulated their imaginations.

These were the elements that could help to produce the illusion that boys were women: an atmosphere alive to what a woman should be; help from the playwrights who did not depict those parts of a woman's life that are peculiar to her; and an erotic literature to inspire passion on the stage.

CHAPTER THREE

To be an Actor

'Nor do you saw the air too much with your hand thus'

Boys would have had to acquire many skills before they could take leading parts. Thomas Gainesford wrote in 1616 that: 'Players have . . . many excellent qualities: as dancing, activities, musicke, song, elloqution, ability of body, memory, vigilancy, skill of weapon, pregnancy of wit and such like' (*The Rich Cabinet*). One of the skills was gesture, which was influenced by dress and boys' movements would be governed by what the farthingale, petticoats and large, bulbous sleeves would allow.

Even though the dramatists did not put the boys in the position of having to act those arts of a woman's life which are pertinent to her, they did, however, expect them to simulate some feminine pursuits, among them sewing. Bianca and Marina sew offstage, but Virgilia in *Coriolanus* has to sew onstage. Katherine of Aragon in *All is True* plies her needles and the queen and her ladies sew in the little-known play *Thomas of Woodstock*. We rarely see a woman directing a household – in *Romeo and Juliet* it is Capulet himself who arranges the wedding feast, and though in *The Merry Wives of Windsor* it is obvious that the women are responsible for the laundry, they do not actually do it. The boys' acquisition of gesture would be confined to learning how to walk, sit and use hand properties, such as a fan, in a feminine way. Gesture is different for men and women, but gentlefolk were expected to do everything with studied grace. Castiglione writes in *The Book of the Courtier*:

If I remember rightly, my dear Count, it seems to me that you have repeated several times this evening that the courtier has to imbue with grace his movements, his gestures, his way of doing things and, in short, his every action.

and later on:

I say that if anyone is to acquire grace . . . he should start young and learn the principles from the best teachers . . . anyone who wants to be a good pupil must not only do things well but must also make a constant effort to imitate and, if possible, exactly reproduce his master.

Anyone, and this means the boys and their masters, could study the meaning of gestures from books. Bulwer's *Chironomia* and *Chirologia* (plate 7), which were widely circulated, together with other etiquette books, showed correct gestures for different emotions. Far from being stylised, these movements have obviously been observed by author and illustrator. Writers stressed that external actions must always proceed from internal feeling and emotion and be true to them. In the unsubtle atmosphere of the outdoor theatres, gestures could do much to project the emotions expressed by the verse, though too flamboyant movements were probably frowned upon. Looking at the small, static pictures in Bulwer, it is difficult to see how the signs portrayed could flow and blend into each other, but in 1951 and 1952 B.L. Joseph, with the actor Bernard Miles and his company, conducted an experiment. In his book *Elizabethan Acting*, Joseph gives a description of these performances and shows how carefully drilled actors were able to use spontaneously gestures that were found in Bulwer's *Chironomia* and *Chirilogia*. Joseph writes:

It is certain that the 'actions' described by such writers as Bulwer can be used validly and stirringly by modern actors as 'the projection of

some inner experience'. . . . The gestures . . . seemed to arise naturally
from the verse.

The critics of the day seemed to find nothing unusual in the
gestures used by the company, *The Times* commenting that they
were not stilted while J.C. Trewin said that they seemed 'perfectly
normal'. Roy Walker, quoted by Joseph, said:

> Their acting was greatly helped rather than hindered by dramatically
> different significant movement that often communicated a sensation of
> watching Elizabethan performers and speech that at least invited us to
> share imaginative and emotional ordeals that were not conceived in
> the idiom of modern experience. Retrospective analysis can catch
> Mr Miles in the stance familiar from old prints, slightly bent forward
> with one leg advanced and knees flexed, and identify the finger-count
> 'the swift, the slow, the subtle etc', as a rhetorical figure, but at the
> time one was primarily aware of the dramatic effect.

The boys would have learnt swordsmanship as well. It is unlikely
that they would need the art when playing a girl – Viola shows only
too well that she cannot fight – but it was customary for young
boys and men to master the skill of fencing and, when playing
young men, as some of them probably did, it would be necessary.
Fencing schools were available and perhaps this was one of the skills
in which a master would see that his apprentice was proficient.

Another grace the boys had to master was dancing, for it was
usual for performances to finish with a dance and several of the
plays end with one. Dancing was taken seriously and dancing
schools taught the art. As Bourbon says of the English in *Henry V*:

> They bid us 'To the English dancing-schools
> And teach lavoltas and swift corantos'.

Beatrice in *Much Ado About Nothing* characterises some of the dances the pupils would learn:

> The Fault will be with the music, cousin, if you be not wooed in good time. If the Prince be too important, tell him there is a measure in everything, and so dance out the answer. For hear me, Hero wooing, wedding, and repenting is as a Scotch jig, a measure, and cinque pace. The first suit is hot and hasty, like a Scotch jig – and full as fantastical; the wedding mannerly modest, as a measure, full of state and ancientry. And then comes repentance, and with bad legs falls into the cinque pace faster and faster till he sinks in his grave.
>
> [1:iii]

Dancing divided into two types: the basse dance or the measure, where the feet did not leave the ground; and the haute dance, the steps of which included hops, leaps and high jumps, where the men supported the women – La Volta being an example. Every dance started with a reverence where the couples bowed to each other. Sir John Davies (*c.* 1565–1618) in his 'Poem of Orchestra' compares the rhythms of the dances with the rhythms of poetry:

> What shall I call those current traverses
> That on a triple dactyl foot do run
> Close by the ground with sliding passages?
> Wherein the dancer greatest praise hath run.

Also:

> All the feet whereon these Measure goes
> Are only spondees, solemne, grace and slow . . .

Elizabeth, who liked to emphasise her Englishness, expected her court to take part in traditional English country dances as well.

Very few books about dancing were published in the sixteenth century – Copland's *The Manner to Dance Base Dances* appeared in 1521 and was part of a French grammar. The Bodleian Library has three pages of dance directions published around 1570, which include steps for three pavanes, seven almains, a tordiglone, a measure, a tarantella, a corante and a balletto for nine dancers. There are also several French instruction books, but, however, none of these books gives details of the style of dance, the carriage of head and shoulders, or even how the arms are used. They only give the order of the steps used. Doubtless, though, the boys practised their dancing and reached a high standard.

The other accomplishment boys needed was the ability to sing, and learning to sing would help them project their speaking voices into the arena. The adult companies expected their boys to sing well, as they were in competition with the choristers of the boys' companies, and the men's companies would not wish their boys to fail in comparison. Musical education in English choir schools has always been exceptionally good and English boys have been noted for their bright, clear voices since medieval times. As Ornithoparcus wrote in his *Micrologus* of 1517:

Galli cantant, Italiae capriant, German ululant, Anglici jubilant. [The French sing, the Italians warble, the Germans howl, the English are joyful. (Author's translation)]

As David Wulstan points out in his *Tudor Music*, the vocal sound produced in sixteenth-century cathedral choirs would be untainted by continental operatic styles and from that we can conclude that the boys were trained to the same pitch as that of a choirboy today. As Wulstan says, the preference for both boy soprano and alto voices over female voices is more widespread in England than elsewhere and is an old tradition. The laryngeal action is primary and the modifications made to it by resonance are secondary. This means that a trained boy can produce a very varied range of tones by easing tension as the voice ascends. It has been found that male countertenors or altos can choose to sing either in the head, or in a bass register, examples being the renowned Alfred Deller and James Bowman, who was a choirboy at New College, Oxford. The male alto produces his high notes by restricting the vocal chords in his larynx, so that only part of them vibrates. The resulting clear, bright sound vibrates only in the resonating chambers of the skull, a different method from singing falsetto, and which gives a quality that can reach the furthest corners of the theatre even at its quietest.

The Italian theorist Zacconi said in 1592 that the voice should be neither forced nor slow but that the throat should be kept open so that rapid passages could be sung with ease. Another Italian, Maffei, said in 1562 that the mouth should not be opened more than it is when reasoning with friends, that the tongue should be in contact with the lower teeth and that a forward jaw position enhances the high tone, making for brilliance. This is apparent in the glass windows of the Beauchamp Chapel of St Mary's, Warwick, where the angel singers and musicians are shown using a lateral opening of the mouth and the natural jaw position prevalent in the sixteenth century. The same is used in cathedral choirs today. In the early modern period a light flexible voice was needed to sing polyphonic music with agility. In 1636, Charles Butler wrote *Principles of Music* in which he divided voices into five different categories – treble, mean, countertenor or male alto, tenor or bass. Two voices belong to boys: the mean which was middling, that is between the countertenor and the highest boy's voice, and the treble. To be able to sing, one has to breathe properly, take huge breaths, to stand properly, that is in an upright position, and to be poised at all times. It is possible for a boy to have a three-octave range from B flat or D below middle C to the G above top C and this can give a boy a more varied and dramatic tone.

Early manuscripts of choirs, such as are found in *The Northumberland Household Book*, list both mean and treble voices. Judging from a correspondence between Henry VIII and Cardinal Wolsey in 1518 there was great rivalry in the search for good boy singers (Wolsey had ten). Whether or not Henry acquired the desired boy, his choir was noted for its excellent singing; the Secretary to the Venetian Ambassador, Sagudino, said that the king's choristers were 'more divine than human'. The Magnificat written by Cornish – one of the composers of the *Eton Choirbook* requires a breathtaking display of vocal agility by both trebles and means, while a high mean voice is prevalent in much of Jacobean music. From both modern and Renaissance examples it can be seen that boys can be taught to sing in high, clear voices that will carry; and great thought and care was taken in producing voices of spectacular ability for the choirs of noblemen and the court.

But the primary duty of a boy player was to speak verse and prose well. His singing lessons would have taught him to breathe in a deep and open way. As Cecily Berry, the renowned Voice Coach of the Royal Shakespeare Company, says:

We know we need a good supply of breath to give voice power, resonance and flexibility. We know we need its power when working in large spaces. We know we need it when working on classical text where the thoughts are long and often span a number of lines; where, if we break that span we do not honour the meaning, or cannot quite twist the pay-off line in a way we want to get the full comedy of a speech.

Berry believes that the breath and thought should be fully integrated, and that the words the character uses, embued with emotion, move the action and the verse. Berry's ideas become even more important in an open-air theatre with no microphones, when to breathe properly to produce sufficient sound, particularly if working with a smaller boy's voice, is paramount. And words took on an even more important role in a theatre that had little or no scenery, no lighting effects and little rehearsal time. The players' understanding of a line, or of the whole play, would be more urgent than today, when actors have the entire script before them and long rehearsal periods. Elizabethan actors would not be able to read the whole play and only had their own cues and parts. Until the cast had read the entire play together several times the motivation (as it is called nowadays) of the characters would be a mystery. Shorter rehearsal time and shorter runs of plays meant that there was little time to consider psychological reasons for the characters' behaviour. This does not necessarily indicate that the characters were not subtly represented, but that the outlines must have been broader, with greater weight put on the speaking of the verse. The playwrights had to use vivid words to help the actors, who had to obey the rhythm and sweep of the line. To breathe with the words, to acknowledge the poetry, to fuse thought and breath would be essential.

The director Sir Peter Hall says that the correct speaking of verse reveals the text: actors must keep to the iambic pentameter, taking pauses at both the caesura – a pause or change of thought that occurs in the middle of a line – and at the end of the lines, breathing there, and if this is done then the sense becomes apparent. He tells his actors that the weight runs on to the end of the line where the verb is mostly found. If the end of the line does not have a full stop then there is an urgency to get to the caesura

to find out what is coming. Hall advises his actors to breathe at
the full stops, the end of the line or at the caesura. The breaths
should be imperceptible. Hall always uses the First Folio text as
he considers this to be the nearest we get to the punctuation that
Shakespeare intended. Other directors choose what they consider a
well-edited text, but Stanley Unwin gives his actors an
unpunctuated text because he feels they can reveal the text more
faithfully. Hall maintains that every line in Shakespeare will scan,
though sometimes a line might need an elision or an extra stress.
The actors – and his advice would apply equally to the companies
of Elizabeth's day – have to find and keep as close as possible to
the five stresses of the iambic pentameter and decide then what
is right in the way of emphasis and colour. Hall likens the bal-
ance between the stresses or beat of the verse to jazz, because once
the beat is found, the actor can play with it. The key words
are found with the beat. If the actor finds the ongoing rhythm,
and does not regard it as confining, then the discipline of the
verse strengthens and enhances his performance. Tim Pigott-
Smith, who has worked with Hall on a number of occasions, says
that if you follow the scansion the sense and emotion works for
itself and 'you don't have to pump it out', while Dame Judi
Dench thinks that it needs a lot of hard work but that 'suddenly it
becomes part of you . . . and verse and thought become one'. John
Barton agrees with Hall:

> You breathe at the end of the verse lines. I myself believe that in
> Shakespeare's later verse it is still right more often than not to phrase
> with the verse line . . . I think such verse is in part naturalistic writing
> by Shakespeare . . . it works. It's been said that's one reason why blank
> verse was so popular in Elizabethan theatres – that it made life easier
> for the actors.

Shakespeare's actors, mainly working in verse would have discovered naturally what modern directors and actors have to find out by trial and error. The iambic pentameter is the most natural verse rhythm there is, corresponding both to natural speech and to our heartbeat. A boy working with an adult company would be surrounded by accomplished verse-speakers, and would be hearing daily this natural and dynamic verse, which, as Hall points out, reveals its meaning by its very construction. The characterisation is there within the rhythm and the pulse of the verse, which Shakespeare particularly, and the other dramatists less skilfully, cleverly adapts to the characteristics of the part he is engaged with at that particular moment. As Patsy Rodenburg, the Royal National Theatre's Voice Coach, puts it: 'The sense is always twinned with the sound.' To quote Hall again: 'Every time there's a full stop, there should be a change of tone . . . on a half-line cue, both the metre and the tone of the previous speaker must be taken over.'

The iambic pentameter has five unstressed and five stressed beats. The stressed beats are absolutely firm and dictate the pulse of the verse. If, as sometimes happens, the rhythm is broken, this indicates to the actor that something dynamic is happening either to the character or in the plot. This in turn signals the same to the audience. The beat conveys the sense to them both, the important words always coming on the down or stressed beat. The Elizabethans went to *hear*, not see, a play and were more attuned to the verse than audiences today who, in the main, see plays either in the theatre or television, or who go to the films, where the visual, it may be argued, is as at least as important as the words. The language of today's plans is impoverished compared to the brilliance of the Elizabethan drama. For the actor in verse plays, the rhythm is his life-blood, intelligence and guide. The iambic pentameter is, according to Professor George T. Wright:

Long enough to accommodate a good mouthful of English words, long enough too to require most of its lines to break their phrasing somewhere, it also resists the tendency to break in half. In fact, it *cannot* do so. A midline pause, wherever it appears, leaves two unstressed syllables on one side, and three on the other. For iambic pentameter, however highly patterned its syntax, is by nature asymmetrical – like human speech.

This seems too simple an analysis, because the thought in the verse can be very complex, and full of metaphor and classical allusions, which are helpful in revealing and creating character. The boys would, of course, be fortunate in having the writer there at rehearsals to explain what they did not understand and, anyway, Elizabethan education was very much focused on the classics, so most of the imagery could be explained. Our attitude to words nowadays is far more utilitarian and mundane: they are used more for information and explanation than for their beauty. There is a whole new vocabulary springing up around technology – and words have become dull and lacking in magic, even on the stage. Elizabethan language was more colourful, more charged, needed more energy to speak it. This means that breath and rhythm were important.

The boys would need to study the pitch of the voice as well. Playing in different spaces demanded the ability to gauge the amount of voice to be used. This might sound trite, but even experienced actors find the transition from television to theatre difficult. As John Nettles said when he returned to the Royal Shakespeare Company after years playing the detective Bergerac on television, the most difficult thing he had to accomplish was to project his voice to the back of the Memorial Theatre. When actors first work in the Swan Theatre they find that they need a different vocal technique from when they work in a proscenium arch theatre. As in an Elizabethan theatre, in the Swan the actors are surrounded by the audience and can talk more directly to them. The boys had to learn to be both intimate and muscular in their speaking – that is, to learn the trick of speaking muscularly and project to the top of the theatre, while appearing to speak directly to those standing near them. Actors appearing in the Swan say that they cannot shout there because the shout gets confused but that the theatre does allow them to be very quiet. The Swan has a roof, of course, but actors at the modern, open-air Shakespeare's Globe have also found that they need a different pitch when speaking there because part of the audience is very close while part is high up. But once the right pitch is found, if the breath underpins the voice, then they have no difficulty in being heard.

There is no reason to suppose that the boys' breathing techniques were deficient in any way and, as we shall discover, the parts were written with their shorter breath spans in mind, so we can assume that they could be heard. Members of the boys' companies had indoor theatres, so the problem of being heard would have been less acute for them, but if the boy singers in Mozart's *The Magic Flute* and in Benjamin Britten's *The Turn of the Screw* performing in the vast Royal Opera House or at the Coliseum in London can make themselves heard, then we can surmise that the Elizabethan boy player did.

Contenders who maintain that boys could not have portrayed women's parts cite the age of the young actors, assuming they were around twelve or thirteen. But boys' voices broke later than now, when thirteen is the average. The archives of Durham Cathedral in the 1560s state that boys' voices were breaking at around fifteen to sixteen, while at Chichester the voices broke at sixteen. The oral tradition at Winchester and Norwich is 'much later than now', while at Canterbury Thomas Bull and Alexander Henley stayed eight years in the choir, from 1561 to 1569, which, if we assume an age of eight when they arrived, then they would have been around sixteen when their voices broke. In the late fifteenth century, boys of Edward IV's choir were sent to university at eighteen *if their voices had broken*: 'And when any of these children come to xviij years of age, and their voices change he cannot be preferred in this chapel.'

Gustave Leonhardt, co-director of Telefunken's Bach cantata cycle, blames today's earlier breaking of voices on a high-protein diet. So, therefore, he argues, in an age where less protein was eaten, boys' voices broke later. A sixteenth-century legal definition of a boy also indicates they matured later than their modern counterparts: a woman could not divorce her husband for impotence until he had reached the age of eighteen for it was not considered likely that he would, in the delicate Elizabethan phrase, have enough ink in his pen until that age. Boys' voices may have been high until then too. It is, therefore, reasonable to state that the average boy player would not embark upon minor women's roles until he was thirteen and would play leads from the age of fifteen until he was seventeen or eighteen.

So the assumption is that the boy players were highly trained adolescents who could fulfil all Gainesford's criteria for a good actor. Training, though, is not everything: it can only produce a polished but lifeless performance. The boy would also have had something that distinguishes an actor from a reciter. He would have needed exceptional powers of observation to portray women's roles convincingly, and he would have had to appreciate the truth of the words he was saying by using his imagination. The theatres were set in a particularly vivid part of London, among the stews, the bear- and bull-baiting pits, near the port. The atmosphere must have fed and nurtured boys' imaginations and helped them in their work. Visits to the Inns of Court and the royal court gave them access to another way of life and tours round the country showed them how other classes of person lived. And, as will be revealed, their parts were skilfully written, so that they would be neither technically nor imaginatively beyond the scope of a well-trained, sensitive boy of between fifteen and eighteen. Such was the skill of the playwrights that nothing was given to a boy that he could not perform.

CHAPTER FOUR

The Anatomy of Speech

'speak the speech trippingly'

It is not known how Shakespeare punctuated his plays. Actors and directors who declare that 'we must get back to Shakespeare's own punctuation' are speaking nonsense; they should be concerned with analysing the pulse, the dynamic of speeches, forgetting the punctuation imposed by generations of editors, including those who edited and printed the First Folio. The director Peter Brook in both *The Empty Space* and *The Shifting Point* argues that Shakespeare's verse is a rich and agile instrument where the rhythm is paramount. He points out that when Shakespeare changes rhythm then he changes thought, and in switching from verse to prose he gives instructions to the actor and director to change pace as well as thought. To Brook the pattern of the words upon the page is symbolic of the changes Shakespeare wanted. Here it is contended that, although Shakespeare wrote in the iambic pentameter, he knew that each character had his or her own pace of speaking, right for that character and that character only. Finding this pace or rhythm is essential if one is to portray the truth of the character, and the very nature of the iambic pentameter means that it is highly adaptable to this use. To take an example, in *Romeo and Juliet* there are two speeches which have to be spoken quickly and lightly – one, Mercutio's Queen Mab speech, the other, 'Gallop apace you fiery footed steeds' where Juliet speaks of her impatience to be united with Romeo.

Mercutio's speech needs exceptional breath control, its dynamic insisting on a rapid pace, unstressed rhythm with every word telling, otherwise it becomes a tiring list of images to which it is difficult to listen. Modern editors who indicate pauses by putting semi-colons at the end of each line have no sensitivity to the pulse of this speech. Many lines have to be spoken on one breath, and in the quotations that follow I have indicated where the breaths can be taken with an asterisk. Different actors breathe at different places, of course, but these marks correspond with the dynamic that seems to rule the speech.

Mercutio
* O then I see Queen Mab hath been with you
* She is the Fairies' midwife and she comes
In shape no bigger than an agate stone
On the forefinger of an alderman
Drawn with a team of little atomi
Athwart men's noses as they lie asleep
* Her wagon spokes made of long spinners' legs
The cover of the wings of grasshoppers
Her traces of the moonshine's wat'ry beams
Her collars of the smallest spider web
Her whip of cricket bone the lash of film
* Her waggoner a small grey-coated gnat
Not half as big as a round little worm
Pricked from the lazy finger of a maid
* Her chariot is an empty hazelnut
Made by the joiner squirrel or old grub
Time out of mind the fairies' coachmakers
* And in this state she gallops night by night
Through lovers' brains and then they dream of love
O'er courtiers' knees that dream on curtsies straight

* O'er ladies' lips who straight on kisses dream
Which oft the angry Mab with blisters plagues
Because their breaths with sweetmeats tainted are
Sometimes she gallops o'er a lawyer's lip
And then dreams he of smelling out a suit
* And sometime comes she with a tithe pig's tail
Tickling a parson's nose as he lies asleep
Then dreams he of another benefice
* Sometime she driveth o'er a soldier's neck
And then dreams he of cutting foreign throats
Of breeches, ambuscades, Spanish blades
Of healths five fathoms deep and then anon
Drums in his ear at which he starts and wakes
And being thus frighted swears a prayer or two
And sleeps again * this is that very Mab
That plaits the manes of horses in the night
And bakes the elf-locks in foul sluttish hairs
Which once untangled much misfortune bodes
* This is the hag when maids lie on their backs
That presses them and learns them first to bear
Making them women of good carriage
This is she . . .

[*Romeo and Juliet*: 1:iv]

The phrases are long, need sustained breath control and a dynamic which is fast and light. Compare this with Juliet's speech where the boy actor would be able to take breaths at the end of lines, as well as at the caesura, but, above all, the dynamic is far more leisurely – the boy has time to breathe (whereas Mercutio has to snatch his breaths), to lean back, as it were on the verse. He is fully supported by it.

Juliet
* Gallop apace you fiery-footed steeds
Towards Phoebus' lodging * such a waggoner
As Phaeton would whip you to the west
And bring in cloudy night immediately
* Spread thy close curtain love-performing night
That runaways' eyes may wink * and Romeo
Leap to these arms untalked of and unseen
* Lovers can see to do their amorous rites
By their own beauties or if love be blind
It best agrees with night * come civil night
Thou sober-suited matron all in black
* And learn me how to lose a winning match
Played for a pair of stainless maidenhoods
* Hood my unmanned blood bating my cheeks
With thy black mantle till * strange love grown bold
Think true love acted simple modesty
Come night come Romeo * come thou day in night
For thou wilt lie upon the wings of night
Whiter than new snow on a raven's back
* Come gentle night come loving black-browed night
Give me my Romeo * and when I shall die
Take him and cut him out in little stars
* And he will make the face of heaven so fine
That * all the world will be in love with night
And pay no worship to the garish sun
O * I have bought the mansion of a love
But not possessed it and though I am sold
Not yet enjoyed * so tedious is this day
As is the night before some festival
* To an impatient child that hath new robes
And may not wear them.

[*Romeo and Juliet*: 3:ii]

A sensitive reading aloud of this speech will discover that though it expresses extreme impatience it has to be spoken at a more leisurely speed than the Queen Mab speech. It will become apparent that Shakespeare never gave his boy players any speeches that were not within the breath span of a trained boy's voice – about twenty-eight syllables seems to be the longest phrase he expected to be spoken on one breath; that the construction of the boys' speeches is more fragmented than that of the men's speeches, with more subordinate clauses, with more lists; that the verse is gentler, less immediate and more leisurely. A player has to ignore all punctuation (as the above speeches have) and go for the rhythm, the dynamic, the pulse of the verse and he will find that the breaths come at easy, natural intervals, for the thought and the beat go together.

Juliet's speech also shows other characteristics in writing which Shakespeare used to help his boy player to give an effective reading of a part. He used imagery that was within a young person's understanding: the child waiting impatiently for a party, longing to wear new clothes. His use of consonants to help create a mood is also very apparent in this speech and helps to give it its urgency without hurrying the speaker. For example, the use of 'w', 't' and a hard 'c' in:

Such a waggoner
As Phaeton would whip to the west
And bring in cloudy night immediately
Spread thy close curtain, love-performing night
That runaways' eyes may wink

and again:

For thou wilt lie upon the wings of night
Whiter than new snow on a raven's back.

Where the 'w' sounds force the thought and pace onwards, the 'n' sounds give a liquidity to the speech.

To strengthen the argument a study of the speeches of Viola and Sebastian in *Twelfth Night* reveals the same disparity in dynamic, though presumably the speeches would have been spoken by a boy (Viola) and a young man (Sebastian) of similar build and looks, the characters 'being born within the hour'.

Sebastian
This is the air that is the glorious sun *
This pearl she gave me I do feel't and see't
And though 'tis wonder that enwraps me thus
Yet 'tis not madness * where's Antonio then
I could not find him at the Elephant
Yet there he was and there I found this credit
That he did range the town to seek me out *
His counsel now might do me golden service
For though my soul disputes well with my sense
That this might be some happy error but no madness *
Yet doth this accident and flood of fortune
So far exceed all instance all discourse
That I am ready to distrust mine eyes
And wrangle with my reason that persuades me
To any other trust but that I am mad
* Or else the lady's mad. Yet it 'twere so
She could not sway her house command her followers
Take and give back affairs and their dispatch
With such smooth discreet and stable bearing
As I perceive she does.

[*Twelfth Night*: 4:ii]

Compare this with Viola's speech, below:

74

Viola
* A blank my lord * she never told her love
But let concealment like a worm i'th' blood
Feed on her damask cheek * she pined in thought *
And with a green and yellow melancholy
She sat like patience on a monument
Smiling at grief * was not this love indeed
We men may say more swear more but indeed
Our shows are more than will * for still we prove
Much in our vows but little in our love.

[*Twelfth Night*: 2:v]

This is an altogether more gentle dynamic, more suited to a boy's capacity, while the liquid sounding 'ms' and 'ns' help to shape the sense.

But, of course, Shakespeare wrote children's parts as well as women's parts and by looking at two of these, Arthur in *King John* and Mote in *Love's Labour's Lost*, perhaps more can be learnt about the breathing patterns created for the boys, and it can be shown how a boy with a trained voice would be able to follow Shakespeare's carefully crafted verse easily.

Arthur
* Have you the heart * when your head did but ache
I knit my handkerchief about your brows
The best I had * a princess wrought it me
And I did never ask it you again
* And with my hand at midnight held your head
* And like the watchful minutes to the hour
Still and anon cheered up the heavy time
Saying * what lack you and where lies your grief
* Or what good love may I perform for you
* Many a poor man's son would have lain still

And ne'er have spoke a loving word to you
* But you at your sick service had a prince
* Nay you may think my love was crafty love
And called it cunning do an if you will
* If heaven be pleased that you will use me ill
Why then you must * will you put out mine eyes
These eyes that never did nor never shall
So much as frown on you.

[*King John*: 4:I]

This speech again shows Shakespeare's expert handling of sounds to make thoughts expressive. The repeated 'h' sounds give a quietness and the 'l' sounds a tenderness to this speech, while the breathing patterns show the shortness of the phrases to be spoken on one breath.

Mote in *Love's Labour's Lost* speaks prose, but still in short, manageable phrases as is shown in this, his longest speech:

Mote
No my complete master * but to jig off a tune at the tongue's end canary to it with your feet * humour it with turning up your eyelids * sigh a note and sing a note sometimes through the throat as if you swallowed love with singing love * sometimes through the nose as if you snuffed up love by smelling love with your hat penthouse like o'er the shop of your eyes * with your arms crossed on your thin-belly doublet like a rabbit on a spit * or your hands in your pocket like a man after the old painting * and keep not too long in one tune but a snip and away * these are complements these are humours these betray nice wenches * that would be betrayed without these* and make them men of note do you note * men that are most affected to these.

[*Love's Labours Lost*: 3:i]

Again, the phrases are short so that breaths can be easily taken without upsetting the sense. In this speech, too, we find one characteristic that appears in many of the pieces written for women characters – the list: a series of short but leisurely phrases, such as the lists of flowers in speeches by Ophelia, Gertrude, Perdita and the Queen in *Cymbeline*; Ophelia's naming of Hamlet's characteristics in 'O, what a noble mind'; Olivia's naming of her beauties, though this is not necessarily a device which is exclusive to the women characters.

Throughout the whole canon similar patterns of speech for the women characters exist. Of course, today's actresses phrase the speeches in their own way, and being larger, having bigger rib-cages they do not need to take as many breaths as a smaller boy would, and every actress has her own pattern of breathing. But in the following speeches it will be seen that it is possible to break the blank verse, or the prose, into small phrases, capable of being spoken by a boy without destroying the sense: indeed, the speeches seem to demand to be so fragmented. It is noticeable that as Shakespeare's verse became more supple, more complex, so his use of subordinate clauses or ideas expressed in parenthesis becomes more and more prevalent, especially in the women's speeches. A late character such as Innogen in *Cymbeline* or Volumnia in *Coriolanus*, while speaking the most complex of thoughts does so in short phrases; the earlier women tend to speak in more regular verse. It seems, too, that particularly in the earlier plays, the verse for the women's parts is very accented, again giving the maximum help to the boy player. One early example is Julia in *Two Gentlemen of Verona* whose speeches have a heavy beat:

Julia
* Nay would I were so angered with the same
* O hateful hands, to tear such loving words
* Injurious wasps, to feed upon such honey

And kill the bees that yield it with your stings
* I'll kiss each several paper for amends
Look here is writ 'Kind Julia' * unkind Julia
As in revenge of thy ingratitude
* I throw my name against the bruising stones
Trampling contemptuously on thy disdain
And here is writ * 'Love-wounded Proteus'
Poor wounded name my bosom as a bed
Shall lodge thee till thy wound be thoroughly healed
* And thus I search it with a sovereign kiss
But twice or thrice was 'Proteus' written down
* Be calm good wind blow not a word away
Till I have found each letter in the letter
Except mine own name * that some whirlwind bear
Upon a ragged fearful hanging rock
And throw it thence into the raging sea
* O here is one line in his name twice writ
* 'Poor forlorn Proteus' 'passionate Proteus'
'To the sweet Julia' * that I'll tear away
And yet I will not sith so prettily
He couples it to his complaining names
* Thus will I fold them one upon another
Now kiss embrace contend do what you will.

[*Two Gentlemen of Verona*: 1:ii]

In *The Comedy of Errors* the verse is even more regular – one of the scenes [2:i] between Adriana and Luciana being in couplets while Adriana's long speech in Act 2 scene ii is both heavily accented and breaks into two-line sections.

Adriana
* Ay ay Antipholus look strange and frown
Some other mistress hath thy sweet aspects

* I am not Adriana nor thy wife
The time was once when thou unurged would vow
* That never words were music to thine ear
That never object pleasing in thy eye
* That never touch well welcome to thy hand
That never meat sweet-savoured in thy taste
* Unless I spake or looked or touched or carved to thee.
* How comes it now my husband o how comes it
That thou art then estranged from thyself . . .

And so on through the remaining lines where Adriana can take a breath easily at every other line. Even this early Shakespeare had forged a pattern of writing that aided his boys – short phrases, lists and a heavy beat.

In the main, the women's parts are very short, another aid for the boy as he would not have to be on stage for great lengths of time and would be able to rest and recuperate his voice between scenes. One part, though, stretches over four plays, that of Queen Margaret, who appears in the three Henry VI plays [called in the Oxford Edition: *1 Henry VI; The First Part of the Contention of the Two Famous Houses of York and Lancaster; The True Tragedy of the Duke of York*] as well as in *Richard III*. It is an unsympathetic part and one that needs great skill as it starts with Margaret as a young girl, takes her through her middle-age and turns her into the harridan of the last play in the tetralogy. Shakespeare gives all the aid he can to the boy who played the part by giving Margaret a simple breathing pattern:

Margaret
* My Lord of Suffolk say is this the guise
Is this the fashion in the court of England

* Is this the government of Britain's isle
Is this the royalty of Albion's king
* What shall King Henry be a pupil still
Under the surly Gloucester's governance
* Am I a queen in title and in style
And must be made a subject to a Duke
* I tell thee Pole when in the city Tours
Thou ran'st in honour of my love
* And stol'st away the ladies' hearts in France
* I thought King Henry had resembled thee
In courage courtship and proportion . . .

[*2 Henry VI*: 1:ii]

Even as her thought becomes more complex and the verse more assured, the same simplicity of breathing maintains:

Margaret
* Brave warriors, Clifford and Northumberland
* Come make him stand upon this molehill here
That wrought at mountains with outstretched arm
Yet parted but the shadow with his hand
* What was it you that would be England's King
* Was't you that revelled in our Parliament
And made preachment of your high descent
* Where are your mess of sons to back you now? . . .

[*3 Henry VI*: 1:iii]

In her final play, *Richard III*, although Shakespeare's verse is becoming less line-stopped, that is the phrases are riding over the end of the lines, the rhythm and thought are still fairly simple compared with what follows:

Margaret
* And leave thee out stay dog for thou shalt hear me
* If heaven have any grievous plague in store
Exceeding those that I can wish upon thee
* O let them keep it till thy sins be ripe
* And then hurl down their indignation
Upon thee the troubler of the world's peace
* The worm of conscience still begnaw thy soul
Thy friends suspect for traitors while thou liv'st
* And take deep traitors for thy dearest friends.
* No sleep close up that deadly eye of thine
* Unless it be while some tormenting dream
Affrights thee with a hell of ugly devils
* Thou elvish-marked abortive rooting hog
* Thou that was sealed in thy nativity
The slave of nature and the son of hell
* Thou slander of thy heavy mother's womb
Thou loathed issue of thy father's loins
Thou rag of honour * thou detested . . .

[*Richard III*: 1:iii]

By the time he wrote *The Merchant of Venice*, Shakespeare had learnt to write from half line to half line, that is the pause at the end of the line is less pronounced and the sense of the sentences can run from the caesura to either the caesura in the following line or to the line end. Portia's speech shows this:

Portia
* I pray you tarry * pause a day or two
Before you hazard for in choosing wrong
I lose your company * therefore bear awhile
There's something tells me but it is not love

I would not lose you * and you know yourself
Hate counsels not in such quality
* But lest you should not understand me well
And yet a maiden has no tongue but thought
* I would detain you here some month or two
Before you venture for me * I could teach you
How to choose but then I am foresworn
* So will I never be so you may miss me
But if you do you'll make me wish a sin
That I had been foresworn * beshrew your eyes
They have o'erlooked me and divided me
One half of me is yours the other half yours
* Mine own I would say but if mine then yours
And so all yours * o these naughty times
Puts bars between owner and their rights
And so though yours not yours * prove it so
Let fortune go to hell for it not I
I speak too long * but 'tis to piece the time
To eke it and to draw it out in length
To stay you from election.

[The Merchant of Venice: 3:I]

Here the alliteration helps the mood of the speech. Each emotion Portia undergoes has its own pattern and speed. Portia is among the comedy heroines that speaks prose as well as verse and, here again, Shakespeare takes care that the lines are within a boy's capacity. The sentences are broken into short phrases, and phrases contain no more than twenty-six syllables, the equivalent of two-and-a-half lines of blank verse.

Portia
* If to do were as easy to know what were good to do chapels had been churches * and poor men's cottages prince's palaces * it is a good

divine that follows his own instructions * I can easier teach twenty what were good than be one of the twenty to follow mine own teaching * The brain may devise laws for the blood but a hot temper leaps o'er a cold decree * such a hare is madness the youth to skip o'er the meshes of good counsel the cripple* but this reasoning is not in the fashion to choose me a husband . . .

[*The Merchant of Venice*: 1:i]

Another prose example is found in *Much Ado about Nothing* when Beatrice says:

Beatrice
* Princes and counties * surely a princely testimony a goodly count Count Comfit a sweet gallant surely * o that I were a man for his sake * but manhood is melted into courtesies valour into compliment * and men are only turned into tongue and trim ones too * he is now as valiant as Hercules that only tells a lie and swears it * I cannot be a man with wishing therefore I will die a woman with grieving.

[*Much Ado about Nothing*: 4:ii]

And Rosalind in *As You Like It* also speaks mainly in prose:

Rosalind
* It is not the fashion to see the lady in the epilogue but * it is no more unhandsome than to see the lord the prologue * if it be true that a good wine needs no bush * 'tis true that a good play needs no epilogue yet to good wine they do use good bushes * and good plays prove the better by the help of good epilogues * what a case am I in then that am neither a good epilogue * nor can insinuate with you in behalf of a good play * I am not furnished like a beggar therefore to beg will not become me * my way is to conjure you and I'll begin with the women * I charge you o women for the love you bear to men

to like as much of this play as please you * and I charge you o men for the love you bear to women * as I perceive by your simpering none of you hates them * that between you and the play may please * if I were a woman I would kiss as many of you that had beards that pleased me * complexions that liked me and breaths I defied not * and I am sure as many as have good beards or good faces or sweet breaths will for my kind offer * when I make curtsey bid me farewell.

[*As You Like It*: Epilogue]

Compare this with Orlando's speech in the same play where the breathing pattern is quite different, longer phrases being used:

Orlando
* As I remember Adam it was upon this fashion bequeathed me by will but poor a thousand crowns and as thou sayst charged my brother on his blessing to breed me well and there begins my sadness * my brother Jacques he keeps at school and report speaks goldenly of his profit for my part he keeps me rustically at home or to speak more properly stays me here at home unkept for call you that keeping for a gentleman of my birth that differs not from the stalling of an ox * his horses are bred better for besides that they are fair with their feeding they are taught their manege and to that end riders dearly hired * but I his brother gain nothing under him but growth for the which his animals on his dunghills are as much bound to him as I besides this nothing that he so plentifully gives me the something that nature gave me his countenance seems to take from me * he lets me feed with his hinds bars me the place of a brother and as much as in him lies mines my gentility with my education this is it Adam that grieves me * and the spirit of my father which I think is within me begins to mutiny against this servitude I will no longer endure it tough yet I know no other wise remedy how to avoid it.

[*As You Like It*: 1:I]

Here the scorn and desperation of Orlando's speech is revealed in long, hurried phrases that mirror his inward turmoil and anger. It is quite different phraseology than that which is found in the girls' speeches.

A further example of longer phrases is found in another comedy, *Twelfth Night*, where Antonio speaks passionately, again taking but few breaths:

Antonio
* Orsino noble sir
Be pleased that I shake off these names you give me
Antonio never yet was thief or pirate
Though I confess on base and ground enough
Orsino's enemy * a witchcraft drew me hither
That most ingrateful boy there by your side
From the rude sea's enraged and foamy mouth
I did redeem a wreck past hope he was
His life I gave him and did thereto add
My love without retention * for his sake
Did I expose myself pure for his love
Into the danger of this adverse town
Drew to defend him when he was beset
Where being apprehended his false cunning
Not meaning to partake with me in danger
* Taught him to face me out of his acquaintance
And grew a twenty years' removed thing
While one would wink denied me my own purse
Which I had recommended to his use
Not half an hour before.

[*Twelfth Night*: 5:i]

The beat is urgent, the phrases long, needing sustained breath to maintain Antonio's urgent pleading for his life. The piece needs pace which dictates a sustained breathing pattern.

One of the longest speeches Shakespeare ever gave to his boys in a comedy is Kate's last in *The Taming of the Shrew*. Again this has a regular, easy breath pattern where breaths can be taken at every other line:

> *Katherine*
> * Fie fie unknit that threat'ning unkind brow
> * And dart not scornful looks from those eyes
> To wound thy lord, thy king, thy governor
> * It blots thy beauty as frosts do bite the meads
> Confounds thy fame as whirlwinds shake fair buds
> * And in no sense is meet or amiable
> * A woman moved is like a fountain troubled
> Muddy ill-seeming thick bereft of beauty
> * And while it is so none so dry or thirsty
> Will deign to sip or touch one drop of it
> * Thy husband is thy lord, thy life, thy keeper
> Thy head thy sovereign one who cares for thee
> * And for thy maintenance commits his body
> To painful labour both by sea and land
> * To watch the night in storms the day in cold
> Whilst thou liest warm at home . . .
>
> [*The Taming of the Shrew*: 5:ii]

And so on throughout the speech, which also contains other characteristics of the boys' speeches – a list, spaciousness for thought and breath, and alliteration to help the thought. These, then, are the principal qualities which are found in the speeches made by the early heroines. It has not been possible in the space available to write about every speech, but the principles remain the same. In every speech the boy has room to explore the thought because the phraseology, even when the thought is passionate, enables him to breathe easily and adequately. The pace and dynamic is different from that found in the men's speeches even in the same plays. The thought and structure grow more complex as Shakespeare becomes more assured in his writing, but nowhere does he ever forget the smaller breathing capacity of the boys who created these parts. The same principles apply to his tragic heroines and those who appear in the so-called 'Problem Plays' – *Measure for Measure, Troilus and Cressida, All's Well That Ends Well*.

In most of the tragedies the women play a far less important role, their parts being, in the main, subordinate to the men in length though pivotal in action. The verse takes on a more measured pace and dynamic and becomes less end-stopped and very flexible. This, of course, helps the actor and many of the speeches become like arias. Ophelia's at the end of the Nunnery scene in *Hamlet* is one. (See Appendix 1 where it is punctuated according to the interpretations given it by various editors.) Here it is punctuated by the need to breathe:

Ophelia
* O what a noble mind is here o'erthrown
* Th' courtier's soldier's scholar's eye tongue sword
Th'expectancy and the rose of the fair state
* The glass of fashion and the mould of form
Th'observed of all observers quite quite down
* And I of ladies most deject and wretched
That sucked the honey of his music vows
* Now see that noble and most sovereign reason
Like sweet bell jangled out of tune and harsh

* That unmatched form and feature of blown youth
Blasted with ecstasy * O woe is me
To see what I have seen see what I see.

[Hamlet: 3:i]

Here the breathing pattern is regular and the dynamic measured. Gertrude's long speech, 'There is a willow', is more complex though, here again, we see regular features which pervade the boys' speeches – the two-and-a-half line breath span, subordinate clauses and a leisurely pace which is also helped in this speech by the liquid soft consonants of 'l', 'm' and 'n' as well as in the long vowels of 'ee', 'ai', 'oh', and 'oo'.

Gertrude
* There is a willow grows aslant a brook
That shows his hoar leaves in a glassy stream
* There with fantastic garlands did she make
Of crow-flowers nettles daisies and long purples
* That liberal shepherds give a grosser name
But our cold maids do dead men's fingers call them
* There on the pendant boughs her crownet weeds
Clamb'ring to hang * an envious sliver broke
When down the weedy trophies and herself
Flee in the weeping brook * her clothes spread wide
And mermaid-like a while they bore her up
Which time she chanted snatches of old tunes
* As one incapable of her own distress
Or like a creature native and endured
Unto that element * but long it could not be
* Till that her heavy with their drink
Pulled the poor wretch from her melodious lay
To muddy death.

[Hamlet: 4:vii]

Compare this with the totally different dynamic of this speech by Claudius:

Claudius
* O my offence is rank it smell to heaven
It hath the primal eldest curse upon't
A brother's murder pray I cannot
Though inclination be as sharp as will
My stronger guilt defeats my strong intent
* And like a man to double business bound
I stand in pause where I shall first begin
And both neglect * what if this cursed hand
Were thicker than itself with brother's blood
Is there not rain enough in the sweet heavens
To wash it white as snow * whereto serves mercy
But to confront the visage of offence
And what's in prayer but this twofold force
To be forestalled ere we come to fall
Or pardoned being down * then I'll look up
My fault is passed but o what form of prayer
Can serve my turn forgive me my foul murder
* That cannot be since I am still possessed
Of those effects for which I did the murder
My crown my own ambition and my queen . . .

[*Hamlet*: 3:iii]

This is a different dynamic, a more urgent feel from that in the speeches for Ophelia and Gertrude. All these speeches express passionate, deep feelings, but the women's speeches have a more stately, measured rhythm. (This contention holds as well for many of the smaller male parts, as was shown by the quotation from Antonio in *Twelfth Night* (on page 85.)

These two male characters' speeches can also be compared with Cressida's in *Troilus and Cressida*:

Cressida
* Hard to seem won but I was won my lord
With the first glance that ever * pardon me
If I confess much you will play the tyrant
* I love you now but till now not so much
But I may master it * in faith I lie
* My thoughts were like unbridled children grown
Too headstrong for their mother * see we fools
Why have I blabbed who shall be true to us
When we are so unsecret to ourselves
* But though I loved you well I wooed you not
* And yet in good faith I wished myself a man
Or that we women had men's privilege
Of speaking first * sweet bid me hold my tongue
For in this rapture I shall surely speak
The thing I shall repent * see see your silence
Cunning in dumbness in my weakness draws
My soul of counsel from me to stop my mouth.

[*Troilus and Cressida*: 3:ii]

or Isabella in *Measure for Measure:*

Isabella
* To whom should I complain did I tell this
Who would believe me * o perilous mouth
That bear in them one and the self-same tongue
Either of condemnation nor aproof
* Bidding the law make curtsey to their will
Hooking both right and wrong to th'appetite

To follow as it draws * I'll to my brother
* Though he hath fall'n by prompture of the blood
Yet hath he in him such a mind of honour
* That had he twenty heads to tender down
On twenty bloody blocks he'd yield them up
* Before his sister should her body stoop
To such abhorred pollution
* Then Isabel live chaste and brother die
More than our brother is our chastity
* I'll tell him yet of Angelo's request
And fit his mind to death for his soul's rest.

[*Measure for Measure*: 3:i]

These two speeches, totally different in emotion, have many things in common: a fragmented structure; short, easily managed phrases; one thought piling on top of another – a list, in fact, of short, pungent ideas, easily punctuated by breaths. With Desdemona, too, we find the same type of construction. Before the Senate, she declares:

Desdemona
* That I did love the Moor to live with him
My downright violence and storm of fortunes
May trumpet to the world * my heart's subdued
Even to the very quality of my lord
* I saw Othello's visage in my mind
* And to his honours and his valiant parts
Did I my soul and fortunes consecrate
So that * dear lords if I be left behind
A moth of peace and he go to the wars
* The rites for why I love him are bereft me

And I a heavy interim shall support
By his dear absence * let me go with him

[*Othello*: 1:ii]

Here again Shakespeare helps his young protagonist with sound. Using the liquid 'l' and the softness of 'n' and 'm' to express Desdemona's love, he contrasts these sounds with harder ones such as 'r' and 'd' to show her determination. The same short phrases used by Desdemona mark Helena's speeches in *All's Well That Ends Well*:

Helena
* O were that all I think not on my father
And these great tears grace his remembrance more
Than those I shed for him * what was he like
I have forgot him * my imagination
Carries no favour in't but Bertram's
I am undone * there is no living none
If Bertram be away * 'twere all one
That I should love a bright particular star
And think to wed it * he is so above me
In his bright radiance and collateral light
Must I be comforted not in his sphere
* Th'ambition in my love thus plagues itself
The hind that would be mated by the lion
Must die for love * 'twas pretty though a plague
To see him every hour * to sit and draw
His arched brows his hawking eye his curls
In our heart's table * a heart too capable
Of every line and trick of his sweet favour
* But now he's gone and my idolatrous fancy
Must sanctify his relics.

[*All's Well That Ends Well*: 1:i]

By this time in his career – the early years of the seventeenth century – Shakespeare's verse is so supple that thoughts often tumble from half line to half line, thus giving the actor the option of a more varied breathing pattern.

In *King Lear* we have three sisters, of whom Goneril is arguably the most vigorous. Her speech to Lear in Act 1 is full of pulsating energy, which Shakespeare creates by using the hissing consonant 's' and short, sharp words in succession, as in 'In rank and not-to-be-endured riots' where the hard consonants thrust the words and thought forward.

Goneril
* Not only sir this your all-licensed fool
But other of your insolent retinue
Do hourly carp and quarrel * a breaking forth
In rank and not-to-be-endured riots * sir
I had thought by making this well known unto you
To have found safe redress * but now grow fearful
By what yourself too late have spoke and done
That you protect this course * and put it on
By your allowance which if you should the fault
Would not 'scape censure * nor the redress sleep
Which in the tender of a wholesome weal
Might in their working do you that offence
Which else were shame * that then necessity
Will call discreet proceeding.

[*King Lear*: 1:iv]

Though Cordelia's speech is more gracious it still breaks into manageable fragments:

Cordelia
* Alack 'tis he * why he was met even now
As mad as the vexed sea sing aloud
Crowned with rank fumitory and furrow-weeds
With burdocks hemlock nettles cuckoo-flowers
Darnel and all idle weeds that grow
In our sustaining corn * a century send forth
Search every acre in the high-grown field
And bring him to our eye * what can man's wisdom
In the restoring of his bereaved sense
He that helps him take all my outward wealth.

[*King Lear*: 4:iii]

Lady Macbeth has some of the longest and most complex speeches of all Shakespeare's women characters, yet, here again, the phrasing is well within a boy's smaller breathing capacity. There is only room for one example but examination of all her speeches uncovers a similar pattern of breathing.

Lady Macbeth
. . . * the raven himself is hoarse
That croaks the fatal entrance of Duncan
Under my battlements * come you spirits
That tend on mortal thoughts unsex me here
And fill me from the crown to the toe top-full
Of direst cruelty * make thick my blood
Stop up th'access and passage of remorse
* That no compunctious visitings of nature
Shake my fell purpose nor keep peace between
Th'effect of it * come to my woman's breasts
And take my milk for gall you murd'ring ministers

Wherever in your sightless substances
You wait on nature's mischief * come thick night
And pall thee in the dunnest smoke of hell
That my keen knife see not the wound it makes
* Nor heaven peep through the blanket of the dark
To cry 'hold, hold'.

[*Macbeth*: 1:v]

The hard 'c' juxtaposed with the murmuring 'm' also help to convey the sinister quality of this discourse.

Looking at Cleopatra's speeches, again we find short phrases and lists:

Cleopatra
* O Charmian
Where think'st thou he is now stands he or sits he
Or does he walk or is he on his horse
* O happy horse to bear the weight of Antony
Do bravely horse for wot'st thou who thou mov'st
* The demi-Atlas of the earth . . .

[*Antony and Cleopatra*: 1:v]

or later in the play:

Cleopatra
* O Caesar what a wounding shame is this
That thou * vouchsafing here to visit me
Doing the honour of thy lordliness
To one so meek * that mine own servant should
Parcel the sum of my disgraces
By addition of his envy * say good Caesar

That I some lady trifles have reserved
* Immoment toys things of such dignity
As we greet modern friends withal * and say
Some nobler tokens I have kept apart
For Livia and Octavia to induce
Their mediations * must I be unfolded
With one I have bred ye gods it smites me
Beneath the fall I have.

[Antony and Cleopatra: 5:ii]

Volumnia in Coriolanus, who, with Cleopatra and Lady Macbeth, has some of the most complex verse to speak, has some very long speeches which, it might be supposed, make the part difficult for even a mature actress let alone an adolescent. Again, however, Shakespeare helps the actor with manageable, short phrasing and a leisurely dynamic.

Volumnia
* Should we be silent and not speak our raiment
And the state of bodies would bewray what life
We had led since thy exile * think with thyself
How more unfortunate than all living women
Are we come hither * since that thy sight which should
Make our eyes flow with joy hearts dance with comforts
* Constrains them weep and shake with fears and sorrows
* Making mother wife and child to see
The son husband and the father tearing
His country's bowels out * and to poor we
Thine enmity's most capital * thou barr'st us
Our prayers to the gods which is our comfort
That all but we enjoy . . .

[Coriolanus: 5:iii]

And so on through this difficult and long speech. Another such discourse is that by Hermione's in the Trial Scene of *The Winter's Tale*, which, though intricate, again breaks down into short, flexible phrases, giving the player time to breathe. It also has a measured dynamic or natural pulse.

Hermione
* For life I prize it
As I weigh grief which I would spare * for honour
'Tis a derivative from me to mine
And only that I stand for * I appeal
To your own conscience * before Polixenes
Came to court how I was in your grace
* How merited I to be so * since he came
With what encounter so uncurrent I
Have strained t'appear thus * if one jot beyond
The bound of honour or in act or will
That way inclining * hardened be the hearts
Of all that hear me and my near'st kin
Cry 'fie'; upon my grave.

[*The Winter's Tale*: 3:ii]

The last heroine to be considered is Innogen in *Cymbeline*. Her thoughts are so externalised, all her sentences so convoluted and expressed in so many phrases, that the part could be considered very difficult. But remembering Peter Hall's dictum that the sense will be apparent if the beat is properly acknowledged and if the actor breathes in the indicated places, then the speech will fall into place and become easy to say (cf. Lowen, *Peter Hall Directs Antony and Cleopatra*):

Innogen
. . . * O for a horse with wings hearst thou Pisanio
He is at Milford Haven read and tell me
How far 'tis thither * if one of mean affairs
May plod it in a week why may not I
Glide thither in a day * then true Pisanio
Who long'st like me to see thy lord who long'st
O let me bate but not like me * yet long'st
But in a fainter kind o not like me
For mine's beyond beyond * say and speak thick
Love's counsellor should fill the bores of hearing
To th'smothering of the sense * how far is it
To this same blessed Milford * and by th'way
Tell me how Wales was made happy as
T'inherit such a haven * but first of all
How may we steal from hence * and for the gap
That we shall make in time from our hence-going
Till our return to excuse * but first how get hence
Why should excuse be born or ere forgot
We'll talk of that hereafter * prithee seek
How many scores of miles may we well ride
'Twixt hour and hour.

[*Cymbeline*: 3:ii]

The thoughts tumble out, the speech darting from one to the other, showing Innogen's impatience in a perfectly manageable way. The Queen, also in this play, has a similar fragmented speech pattern, but her verse seems more measured and stately.

In examining these, the most important, and in many cases, the longest speeches given to boys, it can be seen that Shakespeare was well aware of the limitations of their technique. With a shorter breath span than an adult they would have been unable to sustain long phrases and great speed. Consequently, the playwright gives them a dynamic that they could compass. In all thirty-seven plays it seems impossible to find a speech given to a woman character that cannot be fragmented into short, perfectly understandable phrases: there is an amplitude and leisure in the writing of these speeches which is helpful to the young actor, as is the skilful and sensitive employment of speech sounds to help express the emotion and the thought. It is also significant that the parts themselves are shorter than the leading parts for men. Always the boys have time to rest their voices. It is rare for two difficult scenes involving a boy to follow one after another. Even Lady Macbeth, one of the most complex of the boys' roles, has frequent rests. Though she does appear in three scenes near each other [Act 1, vi; Act 1, vii; Act 2, ii], her part dwindles later on and she has plenty of rest before she sleep-walks. Innogen and Volumnia have a good deal of time between entrances, while Hermione is offstage during most of the second part of the play. Rosalind, the longest female part, is offstage during the passages with Duke Senior and 'country copulatives'. while Desdemona is absent for most of the play, though she is kept in our minds because the plot revolves round her supposed adultery. Even the eponymous heroines Juliet, Cressida and Cleopatra have long waits: Portia is absent during the Venice scenes, while Viola plays no part in the plot against Malvolio. All in all, Shakespeare took care of his boy players, placing on them no burden that they could not easily deal with, for the skill needed to play these parts could certainly be attained by a well-trained adolescent boy.

CHAPTER FIVE

The Woman's Part

'hold . . . the mirror up to nature . . .'

Earlier, the erotic nature of much of Elizabethan verse was recognised and it was suggested that boys who acted in romantic plays could use these works as a stimulus to their imaginations. Compare this poetry of John Donne with the following sonnet spoken by Romeo and Juliet when they fall in love:

Licence my roaving hands, and let them go,
Before, behind, between, above, below.
O my America! my new-found-land,
My kingdome, safeliest when with one man man'd,
My Myne of precious stones, My Emperie,
How blest am I in this discovering thee!
To enter in these bonds, is to be free;
Then where my hand is set, my seal shall be.
Full nakedness! All joyes are due to thee,
As souls unbodied, bodies uncloth'd must be,
To taste whole joyes. Gems which you women use
Are like Atlanta's balls, cast in mens views,
That when a fools eye lighteth on a Gem,
His earthly soul may covet theirs, not them.
Like pictures, or like books gay coverings made
For lay-men, are all women and thus array'd;
Themselves are mystick books, which only wee

(Whom their imputed grace will dignifie)
Must see reveal'd. Then since that I may know;
As liberally, as to a Midwife, shew
Thy self: cast all, yea, this white lynnen hence,
There is no pennance due to innocence.
     To teach thee, I am naked first; why than
What needst thou have more covering then a man.

[*Elegie XIX: Going to Bed*]

In contrast, these are the words Shakespeare gives Romeo and
Juliet when they first meet:

Romeo
If I profane with my unworthiest hand
     This holy shrine, the gentler sin is this
My lips, two blushing pilgrims, ready stand
     To smooth that rough touch with a tender kiss.

Juliet
Good pilgrim, you do wrong your hand too much
     Which mannerly devotion shows in this
For saints have hands that pilgrims' hands do touch
     And palm to palm is holy palmers' kiss.

Romeo
Have not saints lips, and holy palmers, too?

Juliet
     Ay, pilgrim, lips that they must use in prayer.

Romeo
O then, dear saint, let lips do what hands do:
     They pray: grant thou, lest faith turn to despair.

Juliet
Saints do not move, though grant for prayers' sake.

Romeo
  Then move not while my prayers' effect I take
Thus from my lips, by thine my sin is purged.

Juliet
  Then have my lips the sin that they have took.

Romeo
Sin from my lips? O trespass sweetly urged!
Give me my sin again.

[*Romeo and Juliet*: 1:v]

This dialogue is very stylised, the imagery stiff and stately. An intelligent boy would have no difficulty in acting this, particularly as the sounds used by Shakespeare, the repeated 's' and 'p', give a restrictive feel to the whole piece. An adolescent boy might find the excesses of Donne or Marlowe embarrassingly out of his experience, but here all the passion is contained. In the next scene between the lovers, known as the Balcony Scene, the language is more natural, but still the heady passion of falling in love is expressed in cool, formalised verse, and, of course, the lovers cannot express their love physically because the balcony prevents it. When Juliet, having married Romeo, waits for him to come to their bed, again, though her emotion is urgent and passionate, it is expressed in metaphors that a boy could easily understand, even using the simile of a child waiting impatiently for a party to express longing. We do not see the lovers in bed, but Juliet refers to 'the hollow of thine ear' which suggests the proximately of two bodies while they are speaking their farewells. This is the only time we see them together as lovers, for when they meet again Juliet is 'dead'. Compared with Gaveston's speech in Marlowe's *Edward II*, Act I scene i, it will be seen that the feeling is totally different, Gaveston's being more explicit, rawer.

Gaveston
My men like satyrs grazing on the lawns
Shall with their goat-feet dance an antic hay;
Sometime a lovely boy in Dian's shape,
With hair that gilds the water as it glides,
Crownets of pearl about his naked arms,
And in his sportful hands an olive tree
To hide those parts which men delight to see,
Shall bathe him in a spring; and there hard by,
One like Actaeon peeping through the grove,
Shall by the angry goddess be transformed,
And running in the likeness of an hart,
By yelping hounds pulled down, and seem to die.
Such things as these best please his majesty.

[*Edward II*: 1:i]

The part of Cleopatra is often quoted as being impossible for a boy to play and, indeed, there is no record of it having been performed in Shakespeare's time. Perhaps he decided that he would rather not have some 'squeaking Cleopatra' play the part. Nevertheless, the role was written with a boy in mind. However, some of the same restrictions placed on Romeo and Juliet are pertinent to Antony and Cleopatra, those other two great tragic lovers, too. The only time they are on their own, after their parting early on in the play, is after the battle scene: he upbraids her.

Their love is mainly expressed in metaphor and simile. Cleopatra herself is a consummate actress. Even when alone with her maidens she is always acting a part, and she keeps Antony enthralled by her capriciousness, as she reveals in her conversation with Charmian in Act 1 scene iii. She consistently changes her mood from scene to scene and the whole part is a feast of acting – she is rarely sincere. Even her death is done in 'the high Roman fashion', alien to her own culture. When she expresses her feelings for Antony, again, like Juliet, she employs metaphors and her pattern of sound is also never consistent, each speech taking on a peculiar and particular quality of its own. This change in sound makes it easier to deliver.

Cleopatra
O, Charmian
Where think'st thou he is now? Stands he or sits he?
Or does he walk? Or is he on his horse?
O happy horse to bear the weight of Antony!
Do bravely, horse, for watt's thou whom thou move's?
The demy-Atlas of this earth, the arm
And burgonet of men. He's speaking now,
And murmuring 'Where's my serpent of old Nile?' –
For so he calls me. Now I fed myself
With most delicious poison. Think on me . . .

[*Antony and Cleopatra*: 1:v]

There is a certain amount of *double entendre* here with the talk of horses but said by a boy it could have an added piquancy. As with Juliet, Cleopatra is never overtly sexual in her speech. The *Sonnets* show that Shakespeare could write very explicit sexual verse if he so chose, but for the boy players sexiness is always softened by metaphor or wit.

The lovers in the comedies use this wit to set up a barrier between them and physical love. Three of the heroines (Rosalind in *As You Like It*, Viola in *Twelfth Night* and Julia in *Two Gentlemen of*

Verona) wear boys' clothes while wooing their loves, while Helena in *All's Well That Ends Well* and Innogen in *Cymbeline* spend most of the play away from their husbands, and the men in *Love's Labour's Lost* shelter behind a vow of celibacy. The wooing of Katherine and Petruccio in *The Taming of the Shrew* does contain some bawdy talk, but this is schoolboy smut and well within the comprehension of a boy.

Katherine
If I be waspish, best beware my sting.

Petruccio
My remedy is to pluck it out.

Katherine
Ay, if the fool could find where it lies.

Petruccio
Who knows not where a wasp doth wear his sting?
In his tail.

Katherine
In his tongue.

Petruccio
What, with my tongue in your tail. . . .

[*The Taming of the Shrew*: 2:i]

There is, of course, much bawdy talk in Shakespeare and the other Elizabethan playwrights, but it is mainly between male characters, joking among themselves. If female characters are speaking, then the effect is wittier and softer, funnier because it is spoken by someone young.

One of the most sexually aware of the plays is *Othello*. From the first scene, the language is very direct concerning the sexual love between Desdemona and Othello, and Desdemona herself is very frank in front of the Senate about her reasons for marrying Othello. However, the language is stylised, she speaks about the 'rites' for which she married Othello and praises his intellect more than 'his valiant parts'. She says that she does not want to be left behind because of love, and though it is implicit that she is sexually enthralled by Othello, being in love is what she expresses. And children can fall in love from a very early age: if you are prone to fall in love, you will do so all your life, so a boy could know about this heady emotion. Admiring someone to the point of idolatry is a very adolescent activity.

Being jilted is one of the most painful experiences that anyone can encounter. Though Shakespeare's heroines are often uncertain about the outcome of their love affairs, actually jilting is something that rarely happens, and, when it does, it seems to cause very little real, agonising emotion. Julia in *Two Gentlemen of Verona* is jilted, but she is remarkably calm about it, the greatest expression of grief being 'but it hath been the longest night/That ee'r I watched, and the most heaviest' and, in a later scene, she just cries 'Alas' and then explains to Proteus (she is disguised as his page Sebastian) what Julia must be feeling, thus displacing the emotion.

Julia
Because methinks that she loved you as well
As you do love your lady Sylvia.

She dreams on him that has forgot her love;
You dote on her that cares not for your love.
'Tis pity love should be so contrary,
And thinking on it makes me cry 'Alas' . . .

[*Two Gentlemen of Verona*: 4:iv]

Here the passion, the hurt, is entirely removed from immediacy. Julia/Sebastian speaks not of herself, but in the character of the page, thus removing her real self from the raw passion she must be feeling. It can be argued that Julia is a reticent person and can only express passion in a removed way, though the letter scene seems to show otherwise. It can also be debated that as this is a play written by a young man, Shakespeare himself may not have been confident enough to express women's feelings. Whichever argument is preferred, the result is dialogue easy for a young boy act out. Another heroine in disguise, Viola, is in a similar position in a much later play. She is serving her lover as his page, and she is forced to woo her more beautiful rival. When she does express her feelings, again, she externalises them and pretends that they all happened to her sister. She never rants or rails about her frustration. The poetry she speaks somehow excludes the pain and the intriguing situation lessens it. Imaginatively, the boy can reconstruct the feeling by externalising it and, perhaps, relating it to some friendship he wished for and did not attain.

Helena in *A Midsummer Night's Dream* is also jilted, but here Shakespeare plays the emotion for comedy. Helena expresses her distress in rhyming couplets, which give a jaunty and measured air to the emotion. The lines themselves are very funny and the fantastical situation in the woods is high comedy, which an audience is directed not to take seriously. If treated as real, it would be a very bitter drama indeed, but the expert timing, rhyme and fantasy steer the play away from anything but comedy. This strategy might not have anything to do with the fact that these parts were played by boys, but, nonetheless, this stylisation does help inexperienced actors, who may not yet have fallen in love.

Troilus and Cressida, another pair of lovers, show vividly the difference in the writing of speeches for a boy and a young man. What do we know about Cressida, what do the lines tell us? A Trojan, her father a prisoner of the Greeks, she is left under the protection of her dubious uncle, Pandarus. She has no woman-friend or maid about her. A boy player would understand this sense of loneliness, being away from home and in the alien atmosphere of his master's house. He would be able to relate to Cressida's having to rely on herself and to her eagerness for love. Also, like a boy of her age, she is at the time of life when hero-worship is merging with an awareness of sex, as her witty lines about the returning heroes suggest. She has some worldly wisdom though, and she is cautious about love too:

Cressida
. . . Words, vows, gifts, tears and love's full sacrifice
He offers in another's enterprise;
But more in Troilus thousandfold I see
Than in the glass of Pandar's praise may be.
Yet I hold off. Women are angels wooing;
Things won are done. Joy's soul lies in the doing.
That she beloved knows naught that knows not this:
Men price the thing ungained more than it is.
That she was never yet that ever knew
Love got so sweet as when desire did sue.
Therefore this maxim out of love I teach:
Achievement is command; ungained beseech.

Then though my heart's contents firm love doth bear,
Nothing of that shall from mine eyes appear.

[*Troilus and Cressida*: 1:ii]

This speech, in rhyming couplets, discusses very coolly what a woman should do when she is in love. It is very reasoned, not in the least passionate, and well within the emotional and physical range of a boy. But contrast this with Troilus, also in love:

Troilus
I am giddy. Expectation whirls me round.
Th'imaginary relish is so sweet
That it enchants my sense. What will it be
When that the wat'ry palates taste indeed
Love's thrice reputed nectar? Death, I fear me,
Swooning destruction, or some joy too fine,
Too subtle-potent, tuned too sharp in sweetness
For the capacity of my ruder powers.
I fear it much, and do fear besides
That I shall lose distinction in my joys,
As doth a battle when they charge on heaps
Of enemy flying.

[*Troilus and Cressida*: 3:ii]

This is visceral, raw passion. The contrast between this expression of love and Cressida's is great and vividly shows that Shakespeare expected more from his grown-up actors than he did from his boys. Troilus expresses the sharpness of sex and the depth of his love, while Cressida is coolly calculating, as she is when she actually meets Troilus (same scene: speech starting 'Hard I seem to be won?'). The images she uses throughout are ones that even a child could comprehend. The boy playing the part would have seen, probably experienced, tyrannical behaviour and he would know about mothers and unbridled children. He might understand that, sometimes, speaking out, being honest, could be detrimental to one's well-being. Unlike the comedy heroines, Cressida does not change into men's clothing and, therefore, gain the privilege of being able to speak out and do some wooing herself.

What happens after the lovers are parted? Troilus apparently does nothing to save Cressida from becoming a hostage to the Greeks, which must make her feel even less protected and for once she becomes passionate. But children do know about loss and an Elizabethan child would have experienced loss more than a modern child. Cressida expresses her pain in Act 4 scene v in language understandable by someone quite young.

It is almost a cliché to say that there is no such thing as a happy marriage in Shakespeare, and like most clichés, it is true. Two very troubled marriages are those of Othello and Desdemona and Innogen and Posthumus. Desdemona, at the beginning of the play is very forthright and in her first scene is outspoken, but the words are ceremonial in dynamic and the scene is a state occasion. Throughout the play she keeps a certain sense of the ceremonial in her speeches. She expresses the most pain in a scene with Emilia:

Desdemona
I ha' none. Do not talk to me, Emilia.
I cannot weep, nor answers have I none
But what should go by water.

[*Othello*: 4:ii]

In her final scene with Emilia she again demonstrates no emotion which it would not be easy for a boy to understand and express, but Shakespeare here makes it possible to play the scene as though Desdemona had suddenly become a little girl again, very young and unsophisticated.

Of all Shakespeare's heroines, Innogen in *Cymbeline* has some of the most difficult scenes to convey. She can be played very young, but she has a determination about her that also makes her very strong. Again, these are emotions that a boy would know about, and Innogen always externalises her feelings even in the scene when she wakes to find her husband's (supposed) corpse beside her.

Innogen
Yes sir, to Milford Haven. Which is the way?
I thank you. By yon bush? Pray how far thither?
'Odds pitying, can it be six miles yet?
I have gone all night. 'Faith I'll down and sleep.
But soft, no bedfellow! O gods and goddesses!
These flowers are like the pleasures of the world,
This bloody man the care don't. I hope I dream,
For so I thought I was a cave keeper,
And cook to honest creatures. But 'tis not so.
'Twas but a bolt of nothing, shot of nothing
Which the brain makes of fumes. Our very eyes
Are something like our judgements blind. Good faith,
I tremble still in fear; but if there be
Yet left in heaven as small a drop of pity
As a wren's eye, feared gods, a part of it!
The dream's here still. Even when I wake it is
Without me as within me; not imagined but felt.
A headless man? The garments of Posthumus
I know the shape of's leg, this is his hand,
His foot Mercurial, his Martial thigh,

The brawns of Hercules but his Jovial face —
Murder in heaven! How? 'Tis gone. Pisanio
All curses madden Hecuba gave the Greeks,
And mine to boot, be darted on thee! Thou
Conspired with that irregular devil Cloten
Hath here cut off my lord. To write and read
Be henceforth treacherous! Damned Pisanio
Hath with his forged letters — damned Pisanio —
From this most bravest vessel of the world
Struck this main-top! O Posthumus, alas,
Where is thy head? Where's that? Ay me, where's that?
Pisanio might have killed thee at the heart
And left thy head on. How should this be? Pisanio
'Tis he and Cloten. Malice and lucre in them
Have laid this woe here. O, 'tis pregnant, pregnant!
The drug he gave me, which he said was precious
And cordial to me, have I not found it
Murd'rous to the senses? That confirms it home.
This is Pisanio's deed, and Cloten. O
Give colour to my pale cheek with thy blood,
That we the horrider may seem to those
Which chance to find us! O my lord, my lord!

[*Cymbeline*: 4:ii]

This is a very curious speech and one that any actress who has played the part says is among the most difficult to portray convincingly. Here is a newly wedded princess who has been parted from her husband and who has eagerly made a perilous journey to meet him again. She wakes up from a drugged sleep and sees what she thinks is his headless corpse beside her. Difficult to act indeed, but see how carefully Shakespeare paces it. The first few lines are dreamlike — that state we all know between waking and sleeping when the dream still has us in its thrall. Innogen's discovery of the corpse is still dreamlike, then realising that she is now fully awake she believes that the body is Posthumus's. Does she express any heartfelt emotions? Does she express her grief? No, she describes Posthumus in several classical metaphors and then vents her rage on Pisanio and Cloten, whom, without any evidence, she blames for Posthumus's death. Now, for a boy player this would be easy to act. We all know that waking/sleeping feeling; the realisation of the death is very stylised, and rage is an emotion we experience from an early age; even babies have rage in their repertoire. Only the last cry denotes any real anguish and so the whole speech is arranged to be within a stylised limit of emotions. Again, passion is externalised and formalised. The sounds, too, are manipulated – the soft 'n' and 'l' of the dreamlike beginning contrast with harder, more explosive sounds later on in the speech.

Many of these comments could apply to the character of Lady Macbeth. She is strong with a pernicious influence over her husband, but, again, these are aspects of human nature that a boy could have observed. He might, indeed, have come under the influence of a domineering woman. But Lady Macbeth is one of the few women characters who express a purely female emotion, impossible for any man to realise. The lines:

Lady Macbeth
. . . I have given suck, and know
How tender 'tis to love the babe that milks me.
I would, while it was smiling in my face;
Have plucked my nipples from his boneless gums
And dashed the brains out.

[*Macbeth*: 1:vii]

To play these lines convincingly a boy, or any actor who has not had a child, would have to work by observation and imagination. It is impossible for any actor to have experienced at first hand all of the emotions he or she is expected to portray on the stage, but any actor who is good can dredge from his experience something related to the emotion he is required to show. Although Lady Macbeth is not an easy part for anyone to act convincingly, again Shakespeare helps the actor all the way through with vivid, understandable images. The Lady is not in herself evil, she has to *ask* to be made evil and conjures up spirits to ensure that she can go through with what her ambition wants. In a sense, she is acting a part until her final collapse, where again the language and imagery summon up the feelings that she is experiencing. As with most of Shakespeare, the language and the dynamic of the speech dictate the acting.

Rape is one of the most traumatic human experiences. How does Shakespeare deal with this? Among the reasons his comedy heroines give for dressing as men is to prevent rape. 'Beauty provoketh thieves sooner than gold', as Rosalind remarks in *As You Like It*. In a later play, *The Jovial Crew* by Richard Broome, we do see two girls being accosted by a young gallant and saved by their friends from assault. There is, however, one rape in the canon, that of Lavinia in *Titus Andronicus*, but because she is speechless, we have no idea of her feelings for she is unable to utter them. Spanish contemporaries Lope de Vega (who in *Fuentes Ovejuna* expresses the fear of rape so terrifyingly) and Calderon de la Barca did deal with this subject, but they had actresses to play the parts.

Turning now to what are called character parts, which could be considered more difficult to act, it can be argued that both the Nurse in *Romeo and Juliet*, Mistress Quickly and Doll Tearsheet in *2 Henry IV* are unplayable by young people. However, we know that one boy, Solomon Pavy, could act old men extremely skilfully, as Ben Jonson's poem states, so an old lady or a roaring girl should also be within the capacity of a young actor. The theatres were in the same district as the taverns and brothels, so there would be plenty of women of a dubious nature for the boys to watch and observe in order to incorporate their mannerisms into the playing of these bawdy parts. The Death of Falstaff in *Henry V* is a difficult speech for any actor of any age, but again the language helps to express the emotion graphically.

There are daughters with fathers in the plays, but mostly these men require obedience from their children, something well within the experience of an adolescent who was apprenticed. Juliet's speech on her return from Friar Laurence's cell conveys what obedient children are expected to feel.

In *King Lear* there are three daughters, two who become evil, and a spoilt but good one. Goneril and Regan are utterly repellent, hypocritical, cruel and deceiving. They are almost caricatures and can be acted in a flat, hard way, though much more can be found in the parts. Evil is always easier to act than goodness. The younger daughter, Cordelia, though good, is a far more deeply drawn character. She is, to use a colloquial phrase, a chip off the old block in that she has many of her father's characteristics, being obstinate and, later on in the play, showing the authority that he once had. In the Awakening Scene, too, she shows all the diplomatic qualities that distinguish a great leader.

Innogen in *Cymbeline* is a princess with a father with whom she is at variance and a stepmother whom she loathes and by whom she is hated. The Queen cannot be counted as a true mother and the situation between them is not one of mother/daughter friendliness. The enmity between the two makes them rivals for the King's affection – a situation that often occurs in families but here is exacerbated by the question of inheritance. The Queen is a wonderful part to act and must be relished: she combines real evil with superb poetry and is almost transparent in her villainy; not much subtlety there, as when she tries to suborn Pisanio:

Queen
  Thou tak'st up
Thou know'st not what; but take it for thy labour.
It is a thing I made which hath the king
Five times redeemed from death. I do not know
What is more cordial. Nay, I prithee take it.
It is an earnest of a further good
That I mean to thee. Tell thy mistress how
The case stands with her; do't as from thyself.
Think what a chance thou changest on, but think
Thou hast thy mistress still . . .
. . . A sly and constant knave,
Not to be shaked; the agent for his master
And the remembrancer of her to hold
The hand-fast to her lord. I have given him that
Which, if he take, shall quite unpeople her
Of liegers for her sweet, and which she after,
Except she bend her humour, shall be assured
To taste of too . . .

[*Cymbeline*: 1:v]

In the same play, as has been seen, Innogen externalises her feelings to such an extent that they, though very affecting, are experienced through a filter, the poetry adding to an alienated emotion.

The comedy heroines are much easier to play because good comedy relies entirely on the actor's ability to time a line in such a way as to get a laugh: some actors say that they can actually mark their scripts in the places where they know technique will get them that laugh. Shakespeare's heroines have this quality: laughs can be found in the lines if they are timed to give the audience a metaphorical nudge at the relevant point. Though the best comic actors seem to have an inborn instinct, timing can be taught. The comedy heroines have style, too. They carry themselves, especially when disguised, with a swagger. They have personality, are not shy and are always acting a part. If a boy player could not act a part, then he would not be in the company. Shakespeare's heroines, in both comedy and tragedy, are very often acting, playing something they are not really, explaining themselves to a court, a senate or to judges. They are supreme actors.

It is difficult today not to see these women as fully rounded, such is the accretion of tradition surrounding the roles, though it must be said that directors nowadays encourage a fresh approach to character-isation. Obviously Shakespeare, working as he did with a company he knew well, creating parts for individual actors, stretching them beyond what they thought they could do, kept his women characters within the capabilities of the boys who first played them. There is always what actors call a subtext to be explored, but the surface, with its expressive and alliterative sounds, is always clear and direct. Even if the parts are read straight off the page and acted by people with little emotional experience, they are still thrilling and exciting. Modern actresses may see Ophelia's lack of a mother as her central dilemma or believe the key to Beatrice is that she is an orphan, but these are not necessarily the only interpretations: other actresses can find other reasons to explain the characters' actions. What can consistently be maintained is that Shakespeare wrote these parts within the emotional range of a boy of his day. By using metaphors that the boy could understand, by omitting, very often, direct expression of passion, by externalising emotions, he made them stylised and detached. The language and dynamic of the verse or prose spur the emotion on and underpin the thought. Sir John Gielgud maintained that the verse does it all for an actor. This is not to say that some actors do not embellish the verse with emotion, but the language is paramount and does not need extraneous decoration. The Elizabethans were acutely aware of language. The skilled boys, doubtless well trained in speaking verse and hearing it daily spoken by the older actors, even by the dramatist himself, would be able to convey the somewhat limited emotions that their speeches expressed. The images and metaphors were also constructed to be easily understood.

To help them communicate these emotions, the boys had the iambic pentameter. As George T. Wright says in *Shakespeare's Metrical Art*, the iambic pentameter:

> Can lend gravity, dignity, portentiousness, even grandeur to statements and utterances . . . it usually conveys a sense of complex understanding, as if speakers of such lines were aware of more than they ever quite say, or if there was more in their speeches than even they were aware of. If the language of everyday life or even the language of other forms of poetry seems usually to leave untouched, unsounded, certain depths of human experience, iambic pentameter has seemed for centuries of poets and listeners the poetic form most likely to reach these depths and to make their resonances audible.

In addition, the very sounds Shakespeare uses help to impart emotions. Peter Hall expands further (*Making an Exhibition of Myself*, p. 345):

> Shakespeare expresses everything by what he *says* . . . His characters have an ability to describe and illustrate what they are feeling *as* they are feeling it. So his actors have to give the impression of creating the

text while they are expressing the emotion. This . . . has nothing to do with naturalistic acting, where feeling is paramount. . . .

This is somewhat alien to modern actors, but it was customary for Elizabethan actors. The boys, trained in externalising emotions, would be able to convey those written into their parts. Especially as, when we examine the parts in detail, we find much is not explained about the women. Psychologically there are omissions. The women's parts are very much at random; they do in a scene what is dramatically effective whether or not the emotions and actions revealed there combine with other scenes to make up a consistent whole. This means that each scene has to be played for the merits in it, and the boys would not have the task that modern actresses have of presenting a lucid, sound character.

CHAPTER SIX

The Other Playwrights

'the players cannot keep counsel'

There were, of course, playwrights other than Shakespeare writing parts for boy players. Some of the most exciting roles ever written for women were performed both by the King's Men (Shakespeare's company) and by the other companies in London and, particularly during outbreaks of plague, around the country.

In Thomas Kyd's revenge *The Spanish Tragedy* (*c.* 1587), Bel-Imperia is a short, but vital part. Her speeches, like the ones spoken by the Shakespearean women, are well within a boy's breathing capacity. Indeed, most of them seem to be in two-line spans, as shown by her first long speech. (As before, the breaths that can be taken are indicated by an asterisk.)

Bel-Imperia
* Ay, go Horatio leave me here alone
For Solitude best fits my cheerless need.
* Yet what avails to wail Andrea's death
From whence Horatio proves my second love
* Had he not loved Andrea as he did
He could not sit in Bel-Imperia's thoughts
* But how can love find harbour in my breast
Till I revenge the death of my beloved . . .

Although there is no contemporary record of a performance of *Arden of Faversham*, the play was registered in 1592 and the Quarto edition was published twice between then and 1633. Neither is it known for which company it was written, but it is presumed by scholars that it is one of the plays written for the Earl of Pembroke's company. What is certain is that the part of Alice is complex and long. Alice, who is bored with her marriage, plots with her lover Mosby to murder her husband. It is not, of course, necessary to plan or even commit a murder to be able to act it, and, as in the parts Shakespeare wrote for women, most of the emotions evoked can be imagined from within a boy's experience. Alice is an arch deceiver: she pretends to love her husband while being in lust with the younger Mosby. Boys can know about pretence and deception, but can they know about lust? Probably, for children can be very sexual, but if not, they can understand about wanting something excessively. But does Alice express her feelings for Mosby passionately? In fact, she reproaches him for not loving her as much as she loves him, but in completely non-sexual terms:

Alice
* Is this the end of all thy solemn oaths
Is this the fruit thy reconcilement buds
* Have I for this given thee so many favours
Incurr'd my husband's hate and out alas
* Made shipwreck of my honour for thy sake
And dost thou say henceforward know me not
* Remember when I lock'd thee in my closet
What were thy words and mine * Did we not both
Decree to murder Arden in the night
* The heavens can witness and the world can tell
Before I saw that falsehood look of thine
* Fore I was tangled with thy 'ticing speech
Arden to me was dearer than my soul

And shall be still * Base peasant get thee gone
And boast not thy conquest over me gotten by witchcraft
  and mere sorcery
* For what hast thou to countenance my love
Being descended of a noble house
* And match'd already with a gentleman
Whose servant thou may'st * and so farewell.

[Arden of Faversham: scene 1]

Hardly passion – anger, self-deception and pride are the characteristics of this speech and these are emotions readily felt by adolescents.

Alice spends much of the play plotting her husband's death – again plotting is something children delight in, and, as the boys would be competing with each other for parts, so, doubtless, there was much manoeuvring and rivalry between them. The actor has time to rest between scenes as Alice does not appear again until scene 8. (The play is divided into scenes, not Acts and scenes.) Here again she reproaches Mosby:

Alice
* Ay Now I see and too soon find it true
Which often hath been told me by my friends
That * Mosby loves me not but for my wealth
Which too incredulous I ne'er believed
* Nay hear me speak Mosby a word or two
I'll bite my tongue if it speak bitterly
* Look on me Mosby or I'll kill myself
Nothing shall hide me from thy stormy look
* If thou cry war there is no peace for me
I will do penance for offending thee

And burn this prayer book * where I here use
The holy word that had converted me . . .

[*Arden of Faversham*: scene 8]

Here we find similar characteristics to those used by Shakespeare when writing female parts: an emotional situation to which boy players could relate something in their own lives (a child pleading with its parents); a list of questions to make for easy breathing and imagery; and metaphor that is understandable. Also, there is a skilful use of sounds to convey emotion. Although Alice is the instigator of the plot to kill her husband she has little to say or do in the carrying out of it. The small amount of grief and repentance she expresses is very stylised and formal. Even her speech rejecting Mosby in scene 14 has little of the passion we find in Juliet or in Vittoria Corombona's eloquent defence in *The White Devil* by John Webster. Alice is not consistently drawn as she seems a different person in each scene. The part is full of instant emotion and has to be played pragmatically from scene to scene, using just the emotions of the current scene to effect – an easier task than portraying and sustaining an intricate and consistent character throughout a play.

The women in John Webster's plays are arguably the most complex in the whole of Renaissance drama. They are certainly among the most eloquent, having powerful, dramatic speeches. But, on examination it can be shown that the emotions in these speeches are simple. It is their cumulative effect and the circumstances surrounding them which make for darkness and confusion. Both the Duchess of Malfi and Vittoria Corombona are essentially victims. It is true that the Duchess herself sets off the train of events that ends in her death, but through most of the play she is a suffering, passive figure rather than an active one; the same arguments can be sustained over Corombona.

The Duchess is one of the few women characters who have children, and motherhood could be difficult for a boy to act. But do we see her with the children, playing with them or teaching them to read? No. It could be argued that scenes such as these are not relevent to the play, but the fact that her children, in the eyes of her all-powerful brothers, are base-born does matter to the plot. Being a mother seems to be an essential part of the Duchess's warm and loving character for she speaks affectingly of them as she is about to die.

One of the most difficult scenes for a boy to act would be the piece where the Duchess tells Antonio of her love, but even here the emotions are stylised. Antonio is always aware that he is a servant and the Duchess deals with him courteously and obliquely, with little explicit passion. Her most direct speech is more to reassure him than to declare a great love:

Duchess
* The misery of us that are born great
We are forc'd to woo because none dare woo us
* And as a tyrant doubles with his words
And fearfully equivocates * so we
Are forc'd to express our violent passions
In riddles and in dreams * and leave the path
Of simple virtue which was never made
To seem the thing it is not * go go brag
You have left me heartless mine is in your bosom
I hope 'twill multiply love there * you do tremble
Make not your heart so dead a piece of flesh
To fear more than to love me * sir be confident
What is't distracts you this is flesh and blood sir
* 'Tis not the figure cut in alabaster
Kneels at my husband's tomb * awake awake man

I do here put off all vain ceremony
And only do appear to you a young widow
* That claims you for her husband and like a widow
I use but half a blush in't.

[*Duchess of Malfi*: 1:ii]

And in her next speech she uses a metaphor that would be understandable even to a small child:

. . . This you should have begg'd now
* I have seen children oft eat sweetmeats thus
As fearful to devour them soon.

The two of them depart to bed. This scene could cause no embarrassment to anyone. The subsequent sorrows and horrors that the Duchess endures with stoicism and dignity are written in such superb and graphic poetry that the words alone convey the emotions and are comparatively easy to act. Even the death scene has a fantastical quality in the words and is a set piece, like an aria: style overcomes content. Throughout the play the Duchess is serene and gentle whatever happens to her, and the vivid words themselves, if said clearly and rhythmically, are enough to show character and enable the actor to give a convincing performance.

Vittoria Corombona in *The White Devil* is a far more passionate creature altogether, but nevertheless has her passive moments. Even the most erotic scenes have a stylisation about them that make them easier to act. The eroticism in the scene where she is seduced by Brachiano (Act 1 scene ii) is produced more by the comments of onlookers than by the lovers themselves, who are almost ceremonial in their words and behaviour. Vittoria tells Brachiano of a dream which, by symbolism, tells of her desire for him and her wish that neither her husband nor his Duchess stand in the lovers' way. Like Innogen in *Cymbeline,* the passion is transferred into language. Vittoria is then absent from the stage until the third act, the scene of her arraignment, where she has little to say until she speaks her own defence, which is broken into three parts where Webster shows his mastery by producing images and sounds to create passion, for example:

Vittoria
. . . * for your names
Of whore and murd'ress they proceed from you
* As if a man should spit against the wind
The filth returns in's face.

Vittoria's longest speech, the one that begins 'What have I gain'd by thee but infamy' (Act 4 scene ii), is one of great anger, full of wonderful imagery. It has a driving pulse and dynamic, and hissing 's' sounds, all of which help to convey the emotions of the speech. The images are easily understood – the foxes, for example, and the following lines would have been easily comprehended by anyone who had seen soldiers or beggars limping in the streets.

* I had a limb corrupted to an ulcer
But I have cut it off * and now I'll go
Weeping to heaven on crutches . . .

The final words are very childlike: suffering from some seeming injustice, a child will cry 'You'll be sorry when I'm dead' or as Vittoria petulantly expresses it:

. . . O that I could toss myself
Into a grave as quickly * for all thou art worth
I'll shed one tear more – I'll burst first.

The White Devil has good parts for other women besides Vittoria: the mother Cornelia for instance. She is a 'rant', vigorous in her condemnation of her son's behaviour. An obsessive, somewhat one-dimensional character to begin with, she does have some exciting speeches to utter later and eventually goes mad, with Ophelia-like overtones. Another older woman in a Webster play is Leonora in *The Devil's Law Case-Book*, called by Webster a 'Tragecomedy'. Leonora is a mother of two children of marriageable age and she is a schemer, full of hate, defiance and anger – all strong emotions for a young player to act. The heroines Jolenta and Angiolella, though, are stereotypic young women and should be easy to portray. In all three plays, Webster creates interesting maids – Cariola, Zanche and Winifred are striking characters and, although the parts are small, they offer an actor some dramatic situations. Both Winifred in *The Devil's Law Case-Book* and Zanche in *The White Devil* belong to the pert maid category, while Cariola in *The Duchess of Malfi* is a paler character, having only a showy death to compensate her for a dull part. In many ways, Webster's women are easier to act than Shakespeare's, for they lack the rounded humanity that can be found in the latter's roles. The line of Webster's women is more obvious; they have defined characteristics rather than character. There is also a taint about his plays, a corruption that would intrigue boys in that unhealthy state which all adolescents go through.

Thomas Middleton's women are tainted too. In *The Changeling* (written with William Rowley) we have a play crackling with sex. The heroine, Beatrice-Joanna, is a spoilt, capricious girl, who is not far-sighted enough to realise the consequences of her actions. If she wants something she must have it and, up until now, her indulgent father has seen that her wishes have been fulfilled. But, when she falls in love with Alsemero after being betrothed to Piracquo she is unable to extricate herself from the situation without impugning her own and her father's honour. She expresses her wish for Piracquo's death to the ugly, infatuated de Flores, thus putting herself in de Flores's power when he kills Piracquo. Though exciting sexuality in the men around her, Beatrice-Joanna herself is curiously inexpressive sexually. For example, in this speech she is remarkably cool:

Beatrice-Joanna
* Nay, good sir, be not so violent * with speed
I cannot render satisfaction
Unto the dear companion to my soul
Virginity * with whom I thus long have lived with
And part with it so rude and suddenly
* Can such friends divide never to meet again
Without solemn farewell?

[*The Changeling*: 1:i]

When she speaks of love it is, like Shakespeare's heroines, in metaphor thus distancing herself from real heartfelt passion:

Beatrice-Joanna
. . . * Methinks I love now with the eyes of judgement
And see the way to merit clearly see it
* A true deserver like a diamond sparkles
In darkness you may see him * that'd in absence
Which is the greatest darkness falls on love
* Yet he best discerned then
With intellectual eyesight . . .

[*The Changeling*: 2:i]

Even in Act 2 scene ii where she and Alsemero declare their love there is a detachment about them both and the declarations rely heavily on externalised emotions and arrangements to enable them to marry. Beatrice-Joanna is far more concerned with getting her own way than showing any tenderness in love or even happiness. Contrast her manipulative speech with the real, sexual emotion expressed by de Flores:

> *De Flores*
> O my blood!
> Methinks I feel her in mine arms already,
> Her wanton fingers combing out this beard,
> And, being pleased, praising this bad face.
> Hunger and pleasure, they'll commend sometimes
> Slovenly dishes, and feed heartily on 'em
> Some women are odd feeders . . .
>
> {*The Changeling*: 2:ii}

Here is an excellent example of the difference between the writing for the men and for the boys. Whereas both men and boys speak in a stylised language, with metaphors doing most of the work, the men, as in this speech and the one by Troilus quoted on page 110, the men speak in a carnal and specific manner, which the women characters never do. The latters' passion is always expressed in metaphor and is externalised. Another of de Flores's speeches exemplifies this argument:

> *De Flores*
> Yes, my fair murd'ress. Do you urge me,
> Though thou writ'st 'maid', thou whore in my affection?
> 'Twas changed from thy first love, and that's a kind

Of whoredom in my heart; and he's changed now
To bring thy second on, thy Alsemero,
Whom (by all sweets that ever darkness tasted)
If I enjoy thee not, thou ne'er enjoy'st:
I'll blast the hopes and joys of marriage –
I'll confess all: my life I rate at nothing.

[*The Changeling*: 3:iv]

This is a vivid, coarse, sexual speech, full of appetite, far removed from what the boy player chastely utters. In the sub-plot Antonio also makes a directly sexual speech, the like of which is not given to the female characters:

Antonio
What should I fear,
Having all the joys about me? Do you [but] smile,
And love shall play the wanton on your lip,
Meet and retire, retire and meet again:
Look you but cheerfully.

[*The Changeline*: 3:iii]

In the 'potion' scene between Beatrice-Joanna and her maid Diaphanta, although much of the talk is about wedding nights and sex, it is far from racy. Beatrice-Joanna seems genuinely shocked by the metaphors Diaphanta uses, which can be read without any real sexual meaning, innocently, though some commentators read it as a piece of bawdiness:

Diaphanta
Ay, madam, let him compass
Whole parks and forests, as great rangers do;

At roosting time a little lodge can hold 'em.
Earth-conquering Alexandra, that hath thought the world
Too narrow for him, in the end had but his pit-hole.

[*The Changeling*: 4:i]

Most of the scene, however, is given up to a discussion of modesty and virginity. A more difficult scene on the same subject is in Beaumont and Fletcher's *The Maid's Tragedy* which is far more salacious. Here the humour and sexual innuendo are similar to the smutty, schoolboy humour that is often found in works written exclusively for the boys' companies for which Beaumont and Fletcher also created a number of plays. The scene is amusing and has a certain piquancy, being both bawdy and delicate. Evadne assumes that the maid, Dula, is drunk and repudiates her for her lack of modesty. But, here again, there is nothing in the scene that could in any way be described as difficult for a boy to say, Dula's most sexy speech being:

Dula
* Nay now I'll keep it till the trick leave me
* A dozen wanton words put in your head
Will make you livelier in your husband's bed.

[*The Maid's Tragedy*: 2:i]

As Martin Wiggins says in his Introduction to *Four Jacobean Sex Tragedies*:

. . . audiences might well find a degree of titillation in the sequence of *The Maid's Tragedy* where the bride Evadne prepares for bed. In a modern production, her gradual undressing by her ladies-in-waiting could take on a quality of strip-tease, no doubt leaving the more voyeuristic playgoers disappointed when she goes to finish in off-stage privacy. But such a response was less available for Jacobean performances, because clothes literally made the woman: female roles were played . . . by teenage boys . . .

In *The Maid's Tragedy* Amintor speaks in an entirely different way about his sexual adventures:

Amintor
. . . Why shak'st thou so? Away my idle fears
Yonder she is, the lustre of whose eye,
Can blot away the sad remembrance
Of all these things – oh my Evadne spare
That tender body, let it not take cold
The vapours of the night shall not fall here,
To bed my love, Hymen will punish us
For being slack performers of his rights
Cam'st thou to call me?

Evadne
No.

Amintor
Come, come, my love
And let us lose ourselves to one another
Why art thou up so long?

Evadne
I am not well.

Amintor
To bed, then, let me wind thee in these arms
Till I have banished sickness.

[*The Maid's Tragedy*: 2:i]

Later on Evadne speaks in metaphors:

Evadne
* You hear me right
* I sooner will find out the beds of snakes
And with my youthful blood warm their cold flesh
* Letting them curl themselves about my limbs
Than sleep one night with thee * this is not fained
Nor sounds it like the coyness of a bride
While he is much more direct.

Amintor
I'll drag thee to my bed, and make thy tongue
Undo this wicked oath, or on thy flesh
I'll print a thousand words to let out life.

The nearest Evadne gets to passion in the scene is in the following speech:

Evadne
* Alas Amintor thinkst thou I forbeare
To sleepe with thee because I have put on
A maiden strictnesse * look upon these cheeks
And though shalt find the hot and rising blood
Unapt for such a vow * no in this heart
There dwells as much desire * and as much will

To put that wished act in practise * as ever yet
Was known to woman and they have shown both
* But it was folly of thy youth
To think this beauty to what hand soe'er
It shall be cold, shall stoop to any second
* I do enjoy the best and in that height
Have sworn to stand or die you guess the man?

[*The Maid's Tragedy*: 2:i]

Again, this is a speech to which a boy could relate his own experience, but in a different context – the desire to have something, but then refusing to have it because he wants for something better. This is a difficult scene, but the emotions are simply stated and substitutes can be made for those which might not be immediately within a boy's experience. Later on, when Evadne takes her revenge on the King her emotions are disgust and anger, something that even small children can express and transmit.

Incest is an experience that a boy, or indeed a mature actor, is not so likely to have knowledge of. Two plays have this theme – John Ford's *'Tis Pity She's a Whore* and Thomas Middleton's *Women Beware Women* (which is not examined here). In *'Tis Pity* (Act 1 scene iii) we, again, find the emotion is expressed by the brother, Giovanni, while his sister, Annabella, is strangely unresponsive to her brother's lust. After some conversation that would be quite normal between a brother and sister – slightly teasing, perhaps a little too flattering – she asks whether he mocks her. He declares his passion and she cries:

Annabella
* Forbid it my just fears
If this were true 'twere fitter I were dead.

After further pleading from him she consents with charm and sweetness:

Annabella
* Live thou hast won
The field and never fought * what thou hast urged
My captive heart had long resolv'd
* I blush to tell thee but I'll tell thee how
* For every sigh that thou hast spent for me
I have sigh'd ten for every tear shed twenty
* And not so much for that I loved as that
I durst not say I love nor scarcely think it.

Giovanni
Let not this music be a dram, ye gods
For pity's sake, I beg you!

Annabella
* On my knees
Brother even by our mother's dust I charge you
* Do not betray me to your mirth or hate
Love me or kill me brother.

Giovanni
On my knees
Sister even by my mother's dust I charge you
Do not betray me to your mirth or hate;
Love me or kill me, sister.

[*'Tis Pity She's a Whore*: 1:i]

This is all written in a fine, heroic vein which can be acted full out: it is affected, slightly false emotion, rhetoric rather than true emotion and so is all the easier to put across.

The Lady in *The Second Maid's Tragedy* (or *The Maiden's Tragedy*, the title is uncertain) by Thomas Middleton is another woman who is distinguished by her chastity and gravitas (a quality possessed by Shakespeare's women also). Defending her chastity even unto death, again she is the point around which deep passions surge, but she, herself, remains a serene, still centre. She does, though, feel anger and the scene between her and her husband portrays her in a fine rage as she chides him for being weak. She tries to stiffen his resolution by using a fine line in rhetoric and heroic speech – a wonderful effect, a speech that can be spoken full out with great, but affecting simplicity:

> *The Lady*
> * Sir you do nothing there's no valour in you
> * Y'are the worst friend to a lady in affliction
> That ever love made his companion
> For honour's sake dispatch me * thy own thoughts
> Should stir thee to this act more than my weakness
> The sufferer should not do't * I speak thy part
> Dull and forgetful man and all to help thee
> * Is it thy mind to have me seized upon
> * And borne with violence to the tyrant's bed
> There forced unto the lust of all his days?
>
> [*The Second Maid's Tragedy*: 3:i]

It is, of course, very unlikely that a boy would be in the position of wanting to be killed for chastity's sake, but he would understand about being in the situation where almost anything else would be more desirable than to face up to the consequence of a wrong act, and anger is a strong emotion which is easy to convey. Later, when The Lady is a ghost, the contrast in acting styles needed would not be beyond a skilful boy.

All the parts exercised so far in this chapter have been from tragedies. Let us now look at three comedies, spaced throughout the period – *The Alchemist* (1610) by Ben Jonson, *The Roaring Girl* (1611) by Middleton and Dekker, and *Hyde Park* (1632) by James Shirley.

To an audience watching *The Alchemist*, Dol Common seems to be very much involved in the action and to take part in many scenes. In fact, she is only in nine of the twenty-seven that make up the play. She has few long speeches, though those she does have are full of energy, spirit and explosive sounds:

> *Dol*
> . . . * 'Sdeath you abominable pair of stinkards
> Leave off your barking and grow one again
> * Or by the light that shines I'll cut your throats
> * I'll not be made a prey unto the marshal
> For ne'er a snarling dog-bolt o' you both
> * Ha' you together cozened all this while
> And all the world and * shall it now be said
> You've made most courteous shift to cozen yourselves
> You will accuse him * you will bring him in
> Within the statute who shall take your word
> * A whoreson upstart apocryphal captain
> Whom not a puritan in Blackfriars will trust
> So much as for a feather * and you too
> Will give the cause forsooth * you will insult
> And claim a primacy in the divisions
> You must be chief . . .
>
> [*The Alchemist*: 1:i]

This speech is both forceful and scornful and not a bit subtle. Dol's part has much 'business' for her to perform, which would demand good timing and precision, all within the capabilities of a well-trained boy. Business just needs plenty of rehearsal. The scenes where Dol pretends to be a Fairy Queen to gall Dapper are perhaps the most difficult to sustain, for they must not dive into slapstick but must be kept on the edge of high comedy. They depend on timing, teamwork and plenty of rehearsal. The boy would have to get cooperation from his fellow actors, but then the laughs would naturally follow for all of them. He has to do the business, pick up his cues and feed the other characters who are initiating the action.

Moll Cutpurse in *The Roaring Girl*, by Thomas Middleton and Thomas Dekker, is another character who, though she gives the title to the play, does not appear all that often, the sub-plot taking up much of the action. Moll was based on a real character, Mary Firth, who was notorious as a whore, bawd and thief. The part requires good technique, but has little emotional intensity. Moll has honesty and integrity and, like many of Shakespeare's golden girls, she combines these with both larkiness and gravitas. She is a catalyst to the other characters for she reveals their essential shoddiness. She is also a character who appears both in women's and men's costumes, something the playwrights make quite clear in the script. She wears a saveguard and in one scene we see her discussing male costume with her tailor. In plate 13 she wears a jerkin, possibly over a doublet. Middleton and Dekker are obviously having fun with the convention of the boy player, taking it to an extreme.

The Roaring Girl is among the plays that have more than three women's parts. In addition to Moll, we have the conventional heroine, the lovelorn yet wilful Mary Fitz-Allard, who also dons male dress, and three merchants' wives. The latter have little to do with the plot but play an amusing scene, flirting with the gallants who come to buy their merchandise. This scene gives a vivid picture of London life and also shows how playwrights trained boys by giving them small parts before letting them attempt longer roles.

The last play to be considered here is *Hyde Park* by James Shirley where we return again to three main female parts. The women's roles are more subtle and need more skilful acting than either Dol or Moll. The play is also in a different genre, being more akin to Restoration comedy than the robust Elizabethan city comedies. Already the Stuarts were casting their influence on the theatre and class structure was changing. Earlier tragedy had dealt in the main with aristocrats, as did much of Shakespeare's comedy, and city comedy dealt with the shopkeeping classes. By contrast Carolinian comedy could be largely concerned with the emerging upper middle classes.

Hyde Park is primarily a comedy of manners and so has to be played lightly with an exquisite technique. The women characters are not involved in broad comedy, like Dol, but they have scenes in which melancholy plays a part – sad, but funny too. The attempted seduction of Julietta by Lord Bonvile gives rise to scenes that have to be played with utter delicacy by both protagonists. It could be argued that such delicacy is not within a boy's ability but, doubtless, the young players witnessed flirtations, may, indeed, have been flirted with: an attractive boy must have been subjected to numerous attempts at seduction.

Julietta can be plain-spoken, as here when she repels Bonvile most civilly:

Julietta
* 'Tis not in my power
Or will my lord and yet you press me strangely
* As you are a person separate and distinct
By your high blood above me and my fortunes
Thus low I bend * you have no noble title

Which I not bow to they are characters
Which we should read at distance * and there is
Not one that shall with more devotion
And honour of your birth express her service
* It is my duty where the king has sealed
His favours * I should show humility
My best obedience to his act.

[*Hyde Park*: 5:i]

She does not use rhetoric or metaphor to express her feelings, but speaks to the point.

The part of Mistress Carol also demands subtlety and melancholy but the language she utters is clear and direct. As she says to Fairfield:

Mistress Carol
* You work by strategem and ambuscado.
Do you not think yourself a proper gentleman
Whom by your want of hair hold a wit too.
* You know my heart, and every thought within it
How I am caught * do I not melt like honey
I'the dog-days why do you look so staring.

[*Hyde Park*: 3:ii]

Although *Hyde Park*, with its melancholy atmosphere, is totally different from Shakespearean and Jonsonian comedy it must have been particularly suited to young actors for it was revived by the young male company, Beeston's Boys – officially known as the King's and Queen's Young Company – in 1639.

By looking closely at some of the main women's parts outside the Shakespeare canon, it can be seen that they rarely contain anything that a boy could not relate to his own experience if he were quick-witted and had excellent powers of observation. Are the chief characteristics portrayed by these women particularly feminine? That they include little of the experiences pertaining exclusively to women is obvious. Mothers are conspicuous by their absence and those that are depicted (in Webster's plays for example) are hardly paradigms of motherhood. Whether there is a reluctance on the part of the writers to portray such subjects or whether it was a convention of the time to ignore them does not really matter, for in either case it made the acting of women's parts easier for boys. Emotion was stylised; women characters externalised their emotions and used rhetoric and imagery instead of carnal words. They also used humour and jokiness to express love. The writing of the men's parts embraces carnality and coarseness. As has been pointed out, there is no lack of sensuality and sexual frankness in the poetry of the time, but this frankness is rarely expressed on the stage where there is a reticence about, and stylisation of, emotions. Heightened language (which used sounds to express feelings) and the use of metaphor to portray emotions (with images well within a boy's understanding) skilfully created an effective performance in the theatre and was accepted there. A modern actress will find that these parts are underwritten and not psychologically complete, but this is because they were tailored to a boy's ability, understanding and experience. Many of the heroines have characteristics that are traditionally considered masculine: they are brave, outspoken, think independently and do not define themselves by the men to whom they are related. They are spirited and rarely downtrodden. The donning of men's clothing by many of the heroines gives them greater verbal freedom than if they had remained within their father's houses or behind palace walls. Independence in women was not very much prized in the courtly books or in the rantings from pulpits, all of which seem to suggest that Elizabethan women attained a degree of independence and freedom that some of the literature of the time seems not to acknowledge. The splendid women shown on the stage are spirited beings, parts which must have been fun for young boys to act.

CHAPTER SEVEN

The Children of St Paul's

'little eyases'

Not all performances of plays in London were given by men's companies. There were a number of companies entirely composed of boys and, perhaps, very young men. The most prominent of these were the Children of St Paul's and the Children of the Revels. Indeed, the boys of St Paul's could legitimately claim to be the oldest permanent company of players in London.

As we saw in Chapter One, rhetoric and speaking well were taught in grammar schools and lessons at St Paul's School were no exception. There is some evidence that boys and choristers, who were also members of the school, were performing scenes based on Old Testament stories as early as the reign of Richard II (1377–1400). By the 1560s playgoing was fast becoming a favourite pastime and though the professional players had still to find permanent theatres, the Children of St Paul's already had a regular repertory and a place in which to act. Under their master, Sebastian Westcott (who held the post from February 1553 to April 1582), they had already established a position in London and were entertaining Queen Elizabeth at court, giving even more performances than her own Children of the Revels. This continued, though there were times when performances were suspended, under two successive masters, Thomas Gyles (1584–1600) and Edward Pearce (May 1599–June 1612). (Gyles and Pearce overlapped for thirteen months.) The master had a large house in which the boys lived when they were performing in public, both by singing in the choir and by acting. By this time they had no connection with the grammar school. They were about ten in number and had three hours a day schooling, as well as their singing education. The master was responsible not only for the boys' education but:

> Of his owne proper cost and Charges, [to] provide as well convenient and cleane choice of surpless as also all other manner of apparel as gownes coates cappes and dubletts Chaunge of sheetes, hosen shoes, and all other necessaries, holsome and sufficient diet, holsome and cleane beddinge, wi[th] all thinges nedefull for them and in their sickenes shall see them well looked unto and cherished and procure the advise of Phisitians or Surgians if neede so require.
>
> [Gair, *The Children of St Paul's*, p. 37]

The boys' main duty was to sing the offices of the cathedral, but St Paul's was far from being the dignified, quiet building that it is today. The present building is, of course, Sir Christopher Wren's. The former Elizabethan church was rebuilt in 1561 after it had been damaged by fire. Inside it was very lively, being used as a thoroughfare, a storehouse for timber merchants and having various stalls both in and around the church itself. The stalls were about 12 feet by 6 feet and were occupied by all different trades, among them stationers, dress- and shirt-makers, shoemakers and, as is often seen in Quarto editions of the plays, printers, all of whom paid a rent to the Dean and Chapter, though the Master of the Choir was allowed to have some stalls attached to a wall of his house. The whole yard and the cathedral itself were alive with people trading, buying and selling – even the boys, for one of choristers' privileges was that they could fine, on the spot, anyone

The Roaring Girle.

OR
Moll Cut-Purse.

As it hath lately beene Acted on the Fortune-stage by
the Prince his Players.

Written by *T. Middleton* and *T. Dekkar.*

My case is alter'd, I must worke for my liuing.

Printed at *London* for *Thomas Archer*, and are to be sold at his
shop in Popes head-pallace, neere the Royall
Exchange. 1611.

13. Moll Cutpurse, title page of *The Roaring Girl* by Thomas Middleton and Thomas Dekker (1611 edition). This could be one of the few representations of a boy player in character.

14. Elizabeth of Bohemia by Robert Peake, *c.* 1610. Her outfit includes a 'drum' farthingale and an elongated doublet bodice. The fan-shaped collar would have been held out by wires.

15. Unknown lady, miniature by Nicholas Hilliard (*c.* 1585–90), showing a wide ruff and small bonnet. Both would have been worn by men and women.

16. *The Browne Brothers*, by Isaac Oliver (1598), showing copitain hats and lace collars.

17. *Unknown Woman* by Isaac Oliver, *c.* 1590. An example of androgyny.

18. *Young Man in Yellow Doublet* by Nicholas Hilliard, an example of androgyny.

19. *Unknown Young Man with Ruff.*

20. Nathan Field was thirteen when he was 'pressed' into a boys' company. He went on acting after his voice had broken.

21. Edward Kynaston, one of the last boy players, commended for his beauty. When he progressed to men's parts he was criticised for his weak voice.

22. Detail from Braun and Hogenburg's *Londinium Feracissimi Angliae Regni Metropolis*, showing the Rose and Globe theatres south of the river, 1572.

23. Laurence Olivier aged fourteen as Katherine in *The Taming of the Shrew*.

who entered the church wearing spurs. As spurriers' workshops were very near the cathedral, the boys must have had good pickings, especially as they were known to be persistent in their demands! As Thomas Dekker wrote in *The Guls Horne Book* (1609):

Never be seene to mount the steppes into the quire, but upon a high Festival day, to prefer the fashion of your doublet, and especially if the singing boyes seeme to take note of you: for they are able to buzze your praises above their *Anthems* if their Voyces have not lost their maiden-heads; but sure your silver spurres dogge your heeles, and then the Boyes will swarme about you like so many white butter-flyes when you in the open *Quire* shall drawe forth a perfumd embrodred purse (the glorious sight of which, will entice many Countrymen from their devotion to wondring) and quoyt Silver into the Boyes hands, that it may bee heard above the first lesson.

The cathedral seemed to have paid no attention to the *Homily for Repairing and Keeping Clean and Comely Adorning of Churches* (1562), which said:

Forasmuch as your churches are scoured and swept from the sinful and superstitious filthiness wherewith they were defiled and disfigured, do ye your parts, good people, to keep your churches comely and clean: suffer them not to be defiled with rain and weather, with dung if doves and owls, stares and choughs, and other filthiness, as it is foul and lamentable to behold in many places of this country. It is a house of prayer, not a house of talking, of walking, of brawling, of minstrelsy, of hawks, of dogs. Provoke not the displeasure and plagues of God for despising and abusing his holy house.

The cathedral was also a venue for hiring a servant or even a prostitute. Some pamphleteers even suggested that the boys were also for hire, but then some pamphleteers, as we shall see later, did have homoerotic behaviour very much on their minds and one suspects that their zeal often overcame facts. It was also a place to find a lawyer and conduct legal business. St Paul's, too, was used as a fashionable place for gallants to meet. They used it as a sort of club, walking up and down the aisle, then going to a nearby tavern for a meal and returning to the church lounge during the afternoon. As Dekker wrote, in St Paul's:

> . . . at one time, in one and the same ranke, yea, foote by foote, and elbow by elbow, shall you see walking, the Knight, the Gull, the Gallant, the Upstart, the Gentleman, the Clowne, the Captaine, the Appel-squire, the Lawyer, the Usurer, the Cittizen, the Bankerout, the Scholler, the Begger, the Doctor, the Ideot, the Ruffian, the Cheater, the Puritan, the Cut-throat, the Hye-men, the Low-men, the True man and the Thiefe: of all trades and profesions some, of all Countryes some.

Where did the boys act? Professor Revealy Gair in his book *The Children of St Paul's* gives a scholarly and interesting account of his research into this. It was originally thought that the boys acted in the cathedral itself, or in the almonry house where they lived. Gair believes, and convincingly argues, that the stage was set up in a private house controlled by the master of the boys and with the knowledge of the Dean and Chapter. As it was within the control of the cathedral and on its land, the house was out of the jurisdiction of the City. Gair says the boys used this space while they were a professional company during the 1570s and onwards. The house had been built by a Mr Heydon and had as one of its walls the south wall of the cathedral in the north-west corner of the Chapter House precinct. It probably impinged on the west-side cloisters. A contemporary document says that there was 'One little howse . . . built by Mr Heydon in the lower place Called ye shrowdes wch howse Raynold Chunell Inioyeth by license of Mr Gyles wch howse was built by the Consent of Mr Benbowe beinge then Almner: and the said Mr Heydon one of the petticanons.'

A legal deposition made by Thomas Woodford in 1603 when he was manager of St Paul's says that the play *Old Joiner of Aldgate* was performed in a private house which had been kept and used by the Children of St Paul's for the purpose of acting for a long time. Gair speculates that the stage, smaller than that in the outdoor theatres, was placed in the angle made by the cloister walls, which were parallel with the south side of the cathedral and the Chapter House. The stage itself was approximately 7 feet 6 inches wide, and 17 feet deep into the discovery place, the stage widening as it thrust into the audience. There was a gallery above of about 10 feet in width, in which the musicians sat and which could be used as an additional acting area. There was a trap under the stage which was, obviously, raised. A double door at centre back, with a curtain, created an inner space and, like the Middle Temple Hall, there was a door on either side of this central door. It has also been suggested that the above space could be curtained also, that the area could be divided and that there was a window which could be opened and shut at one side. In one play, *A Trick to Catch an Old One* a visible staircase was needed, but it might have been built specially for this play. It is also possible that scenery on trucks was used to indicate location, though like the playwrights in the other theatres, those who wrote for the boys' companies were adept at using dialogue to describe places where the action was set. The lower cloisters could be used as a tiring-house. As the floor and cloister columns were of Purbeck marble, the playing area would have looked quite handsome. The theatre was quite small: the audience probably only numbered about a hundred, though more could have been seated in the upper galleries.

Where did the boys come from and how old were they? Originally they were scholars at St Paul's School who also sang in the choir. However, by the time that the boys were performing professionally, as we have seen, the ten choristers were no longer at the school but were living in their master's house and had been selected for their musical ability. The master had the power to impress any boy he thought would be talented enough to be a choirboy/actor. As the authorisation given to Gyles in 1585 says, he was empowered to '. . . take upp suche apte and meete children, as are most fitt to be instructed and framed in the arte and science of musicke and singing, as they may be had and founde out in anie place in this our Realme of England and Wales'. Thomas Tusser, one of the boys thus impressed explains how he felt when he was taken from his home in Oxfordshire:

> . . . for my voice, I must (no choice)
> Away of force, like posting horse,
> For sondrie men had placards then
>   Such childe to take:

> The better breste, the lesser reste,
> To serve the Queene, now there, nowhere
> For tyme so spent I may repent,
>   And sorrow make.

and later he wrote:

> But mark the chance myself to 'vance
> By friendship's lot to Paule's I got;

So found I grace a certain space
  Still to remain

With Redford there, the like nowhere
For cunning such, and virtue much,
By whom some part of Musick's art
  So did I gain.
            [John Redford was Master of Choristers before Westcott]

In addition to singing, the boys learnt to play instruments as Westcott's will shows: he left violins and viols to the choristers for their musical education. There is also evidence that they could play recorders, lutes and harps. And by the amount of dancing in the plays written for the boys, it is obvious that they were skilled in that art too.

The boys' age is not easy to determine. It is doubtful whether they would have been younger than eight, the usual age for boys' voices to be strong enough to be trained, and as the Elizabethans ate less protein than we do today, it is unlikely that their voices would have been strong enough before that time. In his will Westcott made provision for choristers whose singing days were over, presumably because their voices had broken (there are several reference to this in the plays) but who still perhaps acted in the plays. There was a tradition, though, for boys whose voices had broken, to receive some payment until they could find employment: in 1318 the Bishop of London provided money for boys whose voices had broken. (Today, when boys' voices break at a young age, cathedral schools find that they have to continue to educate them because they are contracted so to do.)

That the boys sang well is widely documented. Claude Desainliens wrote in *The French Schoole-maister* (1573), 'Harken, I doo heare a sweet musick: I never heard the like' and 'wee shall hear [in the choir of St Paul's] the fairest voices of all the cathedral churches in England' and to 'tell the trueth, I never heard better singing'.

The queen herself was interested in the boys and saw frequent performances by them is well recorded. At Nonsuch Palace on 7 August 1559 she saw both a passage of arms and at night a play given by the Children of St Paul's before a banquet. The boys also appeared at court many times during Elizabeth's reign, giving nearly forty performances during the 1560s, 1570s and 1580s. They were transported to whichever palace Elizabeth was occupying by barge which 'Caryed The Masking geare, and Children with theier tutors and An Italian Woman etc. to dresses theier heades as also the Taylors property makers and haberdashers'.

The first play that we know that the Children performed was by their then master, Redford. Called *Wit and Science* (1545), it was performed before Henry VIII and followed the tradition of medieval morality plays being, in effect, a dialogue between abstract qualities, such as Wit, Will, Experience and Instruction. It contained, as might be expected, many songs, which came out of the action and were accompanied by viols and a quartet of string players. This play seemed to have been revived and rewritten many times, but the presentation of new works, most of them now lost, continued. The titles of seven plays, including *Wit and Will, The Contention betweene Liberalitie and Prodigalitie* and *A Morall of the marriage of Mynde and Measure*, together with classical and historical subjects (*Orestes* and *The Stories of Pompey*), have been found and date from between 1570 to 1582. They are known from court records. Descriptions of scenery and costumes also exist, such as this for *The Storie of Pompey*: ' . . . was ymploied newe one great citty, a senate howse and eight ells of dobble sarcenett for curtens, and xvllj paire of gloves . . . The duble sarcenett maid into Curtyns and Implowid about Storie of Pompey plad by the Childring of powles.'

The performances were profitable for the master. For ten performances between February 1575 and December 1581 payment was £129 0s 4d, this at a time when a good annual wage for an artisan was around £5.

Under Gyles the repertoire of the boys became more sophisticated. John Lyly seems to have been the main supplier of plays. His works are episodic and anecdotal, and again, the skills needed to act them rely on clear speaking rather than interpretive art. As Gair says of one of Lyly's plays *Sapho and Phao* (1583/4): 'It is a play about social decorum to be shown in one's emotional involvements. It seeks to entertain without intruding. . . .'

In *Campase* (Lyly's previous play), *Sapho and Phao* (which the Paul's boys acted with the Revels children) and, indeed, all of Lyly's plays, rhetoric is the main impetus. In rhetoric lessons the boys were taught first to research their material, then make a plan of what their speech was to contain. They actually put Lyly's ideas into practice, some contestants putting the arguments for, some against the propositions he expounded in his themes. Some schoolmasters helped to train their boys in rhetoric by writing plays and there are some similarities between their efforts and Lyly's works. However, he was writing for an audience and so his plays are not the dry compositions of the schoolmasters. In addition, he had the advantage of being able to employ the boys' musical talents.

One of Lyly's most renowned plays, *Gallathea* (1583), is a pastoral and is a typical early Elizabethan romance. Both Gallathea and Phyllida, the protagonists, are disguised and the plot concerns the unravelling of these disguises. While it seems that Phyllida was played by a young chorister, the part of Gallathea was taken by an older one, or perhaps even one who no longer sang in the choir, but was retained for his acting skills, for Phyllida remarks: 'I fear me he is as I am, a maiden . . . Tush it cannot be, his voice shewes the contrarie.'

Another of Lyly's plays *Mother Bombie* (1589), still very occasionally performed, marks a move forward, for it is not an allegory, a debate or a pastoral: it is a play about ordinary people and marriage. But Lyly's reign as sole playwright to the boys was to come to an end. His affected style and lack of real character-isation was going out of fashion and the paying public was becoming more discriminating.

Lyly became involved in a pamphlet war, known as the Martin Marprelate War. This questioned the validity of the episcopacy and could have brought the newly established English church into schism. Lyly and his fellow writer Thomas Nashe were engaged to write pro-episcopacy pamphlets. It is probable, too, that he wrote a play on this subject. As a result of his activity, the Children of St Paul's were banned from playing in public.

By the turn of the century, the Children of St Paul's were attracting other playwrights, among them John Marston and Thomas Dekker. Their works required more skill in acting than Lyly's but, compared with the plays being acted on the other side of the Thames by the men's companies, had simple characteris-ation. This simplicity is particularly apparent when they are compared with the plays that Dekker wrote, often in collaboration, for the men's companies.

Marston's first play for the company was *Antonio and Mellida* (1602). It opens with an induction scene in which the eight boys discuss how ignorant they are of any experience in acting, as indeed they were after the nine-year prohibition. Some boys, they say, must double parts and they all must help each other. They also invite the audience to help them in an ingratiating way. The theatre, which had been largely rebuilt, was well used by Marston, with characters operating on both the upper and lower stages, and in the second act Marston shows off his young protagonists' skills by inserting songs and dances. The whole effect is very much like a masque and the parts are tailored to his young performers, even mentioning their physical characteristics. The dramatic content includes two deaths and the finale concerns a coffin from which a supposed corpse rises. It was an entertainment rather than a play where the psychology of the characters provided the interest.

Eighteen months later, Marston produced a more sophisticated work, *Antonio's Revenge* presumably because, by now, the boys had more experience. It is a typical Elizabethan blood-bolted drama, set in a Venetian court, with several mime sequences, a ghost, a dungeon and conspirators. There is a dance in Act 5 with musicians and singers at the end of the piece and plenty of corpses. This production required seventeen actors, an enlargement on the previous company which seems to have been around ten. Probably some of the boys' voices had broken, but they were kept on to swell the numbers. Rough and vigorous, nonetheless the play offers good opportunities for the style of acting that is possible for adolescent boys whose main work is to be choristers and who are not acting with adults or being trained by professionals in the art of acting. R.A. Foakes, quoted by Gair, says that:

[Marston's] plays work from the beginning as vehicles for child-actors consciously ranting in over-size parts, and we are not allowed to take their passions or motives seriously. Their grand speeches are undermined by bathos or parody, and spring from no developed emotional situation, so that we are not moved by them, and do not take them seriously in the end.

One of the most notorious plays that the Children of St Paul's presented was *The Old Joiner of Aldgate* (1603) by George Chapman. This was – unlike the previous plays, which had been concerned with aristocrats – actually set in the City of London itself, Aldgate being but a few yards from St Paul's. Moreover, it was based on real people and incidents surrounding a clandestine marriage and the legal proceedings that followed from it. The people were easily identified and the play was performed during the court case. The protagonists in the actual affair went to see the play and it became a *succès de scandale*.

Among Dekker's plays for the boys are *Westward Ho!* (1604) and *Northward Ho!* (1605), both written with John Webster. Here the characterisations are more believable and there is a philosophical or moral tone to the plays. Fidelity, honour and jealousy are themes in these later plays, as they are in Thomas Middleton's *A Trick to Catch an Old One* (1604) and *A Mad World My Masters* (1605). Here the characters are more rounded and have real preoccupations with integrity and the right conduct; they could, and have been, played satisfactorily by adult actors.

One of the most interesting of the moral plays performed at St Paul's was George Chapman's *Bussy D'Ambois* (1604). Bussy himself sets a high moral tone and he is intolerant of human frailty and corruption. He has a virtuous relationship with the unfortunate heroine of the play, Tamara, which rouses the unfounded jealousy of her husband. But, unable to prove their innocence and unable to compromise they meet violent ends. It is a full-blooded Elizabethan melodrama with set-pieces for the boys and dramatic but simple characterisation of protagonists.

Throughout all these plays the verse has a strong dynamic and there are plenty of opportunities for the boys to breathe. As with the boys of the men's companies, the playwrights understood the technical needs of the boys and tailored their verse to the boys' capacities. As house dramatists, both Chapman and Middleton, as Lyly before them, could write parts suited to particular boys and so bring out their individual talents. Middleton, indeed, may actually have run the company during the time he was writing for it. He may have chosen to write about more sophisticated themes and characters, according to Professor Gair, because older boys were kept on to play the more difficult parts. This cannot be proved and Gair bases his speculation on references in some plays to 'virago-like voice' and the fact that the voice of one character is spoken of as being 'contrarie' to a maiden's. But, as has been shown previously, boys voices did not break until they were seventeen or eighteen in this period, and there are boys with unbroken voices who have a deeper tone than other boys.

During this late period in the company's life, Pearce, the master, was helped by Edward Kirkham who had had a connection with the Children of the Revels. By now the children of St Paul's were performing for King James. During the visit of King Christian of Denmark in 1605, the company appeared before the two kings at Greenwich where it performed *Abuses* (author unknown).

Another play of this time, possibly by Middleton, was *The Puritaine or the Widow of Watling Street* (1606), which attracted notoriety by being attacked in a sermon. The Puritan element in society had always been against the playhouses, as were the City fathers, and sermons and pamphlets had been written about 'harlotry' players, but it was unusual for a specific play to be reviled. The incident was made more dramatic by the fact that the sermon was actually delivered at Paul's Cross, the pulpit within the cathedral's precinct. It was given by William Crashawe on St Valentine's Day, 1607. During the course of the sermon, Crashawe repeated the usual puritan complaints against the players: 'They know . . . that God accounts it abomination for a man to put on woman's apparel . . . they know that Cyprian resolved *that a Player ought not to come to the Lords table* . . .'. Later he actually mentioned characters in the play:

> All this they are daily made to know, but all in vaine, they be children of Babylon that will not be healed; nay, they grow worse and worse, for now they bring religion and holy things upon the stage. . . . Two hypocrites must be brought foorth; and how shall they be described but by these names, *Nicholas S. Antlings, Simon S. Maryoveries?*

These were the names of two of the servingmen characters in the play, and were taken from St Antling's and St Mary Overys, two well-known churches. The servingmen (the third was called Frailtie) are arrant hypocrites and, though pretending to be pious, are up to all sorts of dodges that belie their seeming devoutness. They are drunkards, liars and wastrels, as is their minister Maister Ful-Bellie. This satire on puritans could not delight what was now a prominent part of London society. Crashawe also attacked the fact that services the boys attended were curtailed because of plays:

> Oh what times are wee cast into, that such a wickednesse should passe unpunished! I speake nothing of their continuall prophanesse in their phrases, and sometimes Atheisme and blasphemie, nor of their continuall prophaining of the Sabbath, which generally in the countrie is their play day, and oftentimes Gods divine service hindred, or cut shorter to make room and give time for the divels service.

That the Children of St Paul's were talented cannot be doubted. The boys were of various ages. In an early play, *The Marriage of Wit and Science*, there is a passage which runs:

Science	What age art thou of, my goode sonne?
Will	Betweene eleven and twelve, Madame, more or less.
Science	How old is the gentilman thy maister [Wit], canst thou tell?
Will	Seventeene or there aboute . . .

This enabled the playwrights to incorporate a diversity of characters, the older boys playing the more sophisticated characters while the young juveniles the lighter, smaller and easier parts. That the boys were successful is evident, for Shakespeare mentioned them in *Hamlet*. The boys' companies must have presented some financial challenge to the men's companies because it was fashionable to visit them.

Why then did the company cease? Well, fashion is always subject to change. What is 'in' today is 'out' tomorrow. In 1606 and 1607 the theatres had to close because of plague and this seems to have affected St Paul's more than the men's companies who had the greater writers and actors and who were able to tour. The boys were attacked and, perhaps more significantly, they lost most of their writers. Marston had gone over to the Children of the Revels, while Middleton was writing for the men's companies. The whole tone of the City had changed too, with the Puritans becoming dominant. Some of the minor canons who ruled the cathedral opposed the playhouse strongly. Gradually the performances tailed off and an unusual facet of theatrical performance ceased.

CHAPTER EIGHT

The Children of the Revels

'an eyrie of children'

The Children of the Revels – at other times known as the Children of the Chapel Royal, the Children of the Queen's Revels or the Blackfriars Children – were basically the choristers who sang for the monarch at divine service in the royal chapels. The choir had been in existence from the twelfth century, perhaps earlier, but children were an innovation during the reign of Henry IV. He appointed a master of grammar in 1401 to look after the boy's discipline and education. In 1420 came the first order allowing the boys to be impressed.

The choir was renowned for its musical skills and the eight (later twelve) children contributed to the quality of the singing with their high soprano voices. In Elizabeth's reign it came directly under the supervision of the Lord Chamberlain and moved with the court around the country, though Windsor had its own choir, so it is probable that the Chapel Royal choristers did not sing there.

It was in Henry VIII's reign that the Great Wardrobe issued black and tawny camlet gowns, yellow satin coats and Milan bonnets for the gentlemen and boys to wear. The boys did not get any payment for their work, though they were fed and housed and received both a musical education of a high order and a grammar school education. When their voices broke some provision was made for them to go to university. When William Cornish became master (1509–23) the boys started to act. Cornish himself had acted with the gentlemen previously at court entertainments and he instigated performances by the boys who took part in many court masques and entertainments for Henry VIII. Cornish was also a playwright though all his works have been lost. The tradition of the boys operating as an acting company was well established by Elizabeth's reign. There are records of the boys' appearances at court and at Lincoln's Inn during the 1560s when Richard Edwardes was master. It was to him that Elizabeth issued a patent in 1561 which stated, among other provisions, that he was responsible for taking as many singing children as he thought 'mete' to all cathedral and collegiate churches by land or water wherever she removed herself to any place or places.

The boys aroused the spleen of the Puritans. In 1569 the writer of a pamphlet entitled *The Children of the Chapel Stript and Whipt* declared that:

> Plaies will never be supprest, while her maiesties unfledged minions flaunt it in silkes and sattens. They had as well be at their Popish service, in the deuils garments. . . . Even in her maiesties chapel do these pretty vpstart youths profane the Lordes Day by the lascivious writhings of their tender limbs, and gorgeous decking of their apparel, in feighning bawdie fables gathered from idolatrous heathen poets.

The master from 1566 and for the greater part of Elizabeth's reign was William Hunnis: Richard Farrant was assistant to Hunnis from 1577, becoming master in 1597; Nathaniel Giles then became master and remained in the post until 1639. These were the men who guided and produced the boys' plays, though their performances seem to have ended around 1613.

It was Hunnis who petitioned the queen about the financial situation of the company. Henry VIII paid the Gentlemen of the

Choir one shilling a day and allowed the master two shillings a week for each child: this was later raised to sixpence a day, plus eightpence a day for breakfast, which was paid in monthly instalments of twenty-six shillings and eightpence. The children's journeys were also paid for, there were fees for special performances (paid to the master) and, as we have seen, they were clothed from the Wardrobe. But inflation was taking its toll and arrangements had altered. According to Hunnis, Elizabeth allowed sixpence a day for food and an allowance for furniture and apparel. There was no fee for the usher (junior schoolmaster) nor for the woman servant who did the washing and kept the boys clean. There seems to have been no allowance given for lodgings when the boys attended court, nor provision made for choristers whose voices had broken, the master having to find clothing and furniture for these young men. As Hunnis pointed out to Elizabeth, there had been no increase in the allowances since her father's day, though prices had increased, and the gifts that Henry VIII had frequently given had not been continued by the queen. The allowance for breakfast had stopped too. Hunnis asked if the children could eat at court instead. His appeal did not succeed: sixpence a day was still being paid at Elizabeth's death, but the breakfast allowance may have been restored. He, himself, received some crown lands in 1585 to make up for his expenditure and, in all probability, kept the fees paid for the children's performances at court, but in turn had to pay the dramatists. It was during Hunnis's mastership that the boys stopped acting: this came in 1584, though that year they had performed at Blackfriars Theatre, which had been leased by John Lyly whose plays *Campase* and *Sappho and Phao* they performed with the Paul's boys – the first recorded instances of boys playing before a paying audience. But the deal came to an end that year and Lyly continued to write for Paul's.

It seems the boys did not perform plays in London for the next seventeen years, though there are recorded performances in Ipswich, Norwich and Leicester. In 1600 the master, Evans, took out a lease on the building which the company had used many years before, Blackfriars. It had been rebuilt by Richard Burbage's father James. The lease for the building was at a rent of £40 a year and, according to Burbage, the intention was to set up a company of boys to play interludes. Burbage also took security of a bond worth £400 – a considerable sum of money. The company was called 'the Queenes Majesties Children of the Chapell' and it was not until 1606 that it became known as the Blackfriars Children. The children appeared at court in 1601; their first performance was probably *Cynthia's Revels* by Ben Jonson, which showed off their skills in singing and music. It also introduced an element of astringent satire, had some political references, castigated modern manners and was firmly anti-romantic. The second play harked back to the rhetorical-type works the boys of St Paul's were so adept at performing. Called *Contention between Liberalitie and Prodigalitie*, it was more a debate than a drama.

When he published *Cynthia's Revels*, Ben Jonson gave the names of his actors. They included the famous Salmon or Salathiel Pavy, along with Nathan Field, who was later to become a member of the King's Men, Tho. Day, Ioh. Underwood, Rob. Baxter and Ioh. Frost. The induction was spoken by Iacke and two other children (unnamed).

The boys might have been impressed against their own and their parents' will, for in 1600 Henry Clifton Esq. of Toftrees in Norfolk complained to the Star Chamber about the impressments of the boys. He mentioned: 'John Chapell, a gramer schole scholler of one Mr Spykes schole neere Cripplegate, London; John Motteram, a gramer scholler in the free schole at Westminster;

Nathan ffield, a scholler of a gramer schole in London, kepte by
one Mr Monkster.' Clifton claimed that these boys and others were
not singers nor could they be taught to sing. The reason for
Clifton's complaint was that his own son had been taken. Thomas
was thirteen, and had been seized from his own school to 'Exercise
the base trade of a mercynary enterlude player, to his vtter losse of
tyme, ruyne and disparagment . . . [his son was] amongste a
companie of lewde and dissolute mercenary players.' The case took
some time to resolve but Master Evans was reprimanded and told
he must not impress gentlemen's sons. This document is
interesting for several reasons because it sheds light on the boy
players generally. Firstly, it indicates that the social standing of the
players was considered to be less than that of gentlemen. Secondly,
the age of the boys, thirteen, argues against the presumption that
boy players were younger. If the boys were impressed at this age,
Evans must have been fairly sure that their voices would not break
in a year or so. The last point is that they were all grammar school
boys and so, presumably had had some acting experience in the
rhetorical plays that schoolmasters wrote for their pupils to
perform.

At the time of Elizabeth's death the theatres were closed because
of plague but James I gave his royal assent to the boys, assigning
them to the protection of 'our deerest wife', saying that they shall
be called the 'children of her Revelles' and that they should
perform 'within Blackfryers in our Cytie of London, or any other
convenient place'. So again the Children changed their name.

In 1604 a new edict made provision for boys after their voices
had broken and the sum for their board was raised to ten pence a
day. The Wardrobe still provided clothes: in 1605 there is an
account for holland shirts for the twelve boys and a suit for James
Cutler, a boy whose voice had 'gone off'.

It was during this period that the company presented its most interesting plays, works that have made their way into the repertoire, are considered among the greatest of this period and are still occasionally performed. They included *Bussy d'Ambois* by Chapman (also performed by the St Paul's boys), *The Dutch Courtesan* and *The Malcontent* by John Marston, *The Knight of the Burning Pestle* by Beaumont and *Epicene* by Jonson. Thomas Middleton also wrote one or two plays for the boys.

The darker playwrights, with their lewd humour and more realistic psychology, soon became the fashion and had an influence on the men's companies. *The Malcontent* was bought by the King's Men, and the playwrights who worked for the men's companies began to write plays with a starker reality. But these plays did not please the authorities, for in 1605 when *Eastward Ho!* was performed and published the writers found themselves in serious trouble. Marston fled the country and Jonson and Chapman were imprisoned. The boys lost the patronage of the queen and instead of the Children of the Queen's Revels they became simply the Children of the Revels. Exactly what was so upsetting about this play is uncertain. The theme is that of the prodigal son, and the central character, Quicksilver, is what we would nowadays call an anti-hero. The son of a gentleman, he is idle and spends more money than he has in fashionable living, and then resorts to stealing to support his extravagances. Imprisoned, he feigns repentance and is finally forgiven rather than severely punished. The repentance is mocked by the authors and morality is certainly not seen as something to be praised. But this tone was a reflection of the mores of the time. The reaction against the work may have come because the play spoke slightingly of the Scots.

Thereafter, the boys continually gave offence, for their plays were among the most innovative and the adult companies soon became aware that the 'little eyases' were attracting audiences of highly educated and rich people whom they could not afford to lose from their larger, open-air theatres. Playwriting became a more socially accepted occupation, Beaumont, for instance, being the son of a bishop and Fletcher the son of a judge. The two most interesting dramatists were Jonson and Marston, neither of whom wrote exclusively for the boys. Jonson wrote a number of court masques, with designs by Inigo Jones, as well as plays for the boys' and the men's companies.

Other dramatists writing for boys included Samuel Daniel whose *Philotas* (1604) dealt with usurpation, a subject about which James was always touchy: Daniel was lucky not to receive any punishment for his work. He pleaded his cause well and claimed his prosecutors had misconceived the play! His predicament was doubly dangerous for he, rather than the Master of the Revels, was at this time acting as censor for the company's plays. George Chapman also created full-blooded plays for the boys. One of his works *Bussy d'Ambois* (published 1607, but possibly played in 1604) with its combination of sex and intrigue still plays well today (see Chapter Seven).

Another play that, like *Bussy d'Ambois*, occasionally gets a performance today is Marston's *The Dutch Courtesan* (printed 1605). Like *The Malcontent*, this play is a satire and is predominantly sexual in content, but in a comic and involved plot. Gãmini Salgãdo in his introduction to the play in *Four Jacobean Comedies* says that it enquires into 'the extent to which physical appetites and functions of man can be ignored or suppressed in the supposed interest of "higher" or more "spiritual" activities'. The courtesan herself is called Franceschina, and Marston gives her a thick accent which on the page is difficult to read, but a competent actor (as Billie Whitelaw was in the National Theatre production at

Chichester in the 1960s) can make his own accent so as to be intelligible to an audience. The young men in the play have 'known' or know Franceschina and the principal character, Freevill, is now honourably in love with Beatrice, who is a paradigm of all romantic heroines. Freevill feels that his previous sexual knowledge can have only good consequences as through it he is now ready to undertake marriage. Although the Freevill character is well drawn, unfortunately the love scenes are very stiff, especially as the play elsewhere has plenty of very amusing sexual talk. The work also deals with self-delusion and the other relationship in the play, that of Tysefew and Crispinella, shows how physicality and sentiment can result in a passion that is true. Franceschina herself has several stormy love scenes with one of the other gallants, Malheureux, where the comedy lies in the fact that he thinks that he 'is a man of snow' but really is drawn to physical sex. The three couples nicely encapsulate three forms of love and sex. The play is also noted for its obscenities. As Gāmini Salgādo writes:

> No doubt a good many of the obscenities with which Cocledemoy freely bespatters his speech are there because of the professional dramatist's shrewd calculation that his audience could stomach this kind of thing with relish. . . . And perhaps the titillatory effect was heightened by the fact that this play, like Middleton's *A Mad World, My Masters*, was first performed by a children's company . . .

About *A Mad World*, performed by the St Paul's boys, Salgādo comments:

> . . . the obscenity is, though less obvious, more pervasive . . . because it is not so closely identified with a single character . . . the scene where Follywit is disguised as a courtesan, for example, keeps our attention constantly focused on the adroitness of the performance, not on its somewhat dubious purpose.

Sexual humour is an element of the later plays for the children's companies. This is in direct contrast to the more sober writing of the parts for boys in the men's companies, which, as we have seen, are rarely unpleasantly salacious. Perhaps the audience delighted in the contrast of the innocent appearance of the boys and the words they spoke. It must also be acknowledged that the plays have a deeply moral purpose and teach that good is better than evil and duplicity. The women's characters in these plays, also, are not drawn in any great detail and rely for their impact on either their wit or their tragic situations. Throughout this period, the writers for the boys' companies seem always to be pointing at the actors and saying to the audience that in spite of the sophistication of the language and the salaciousness of the material, here, after all, were boys of only thirteen or so. These boys were younger than those who appeared in the main parts in the men's companies. There is also a self-consciousness about the writing which makes for an alienating effect: it is as if the boys were pointing out how clever they were to say such things.

The Children of the Revels continued to be in trouble. In 1606 *The Isle of Gulls*, written by John Day, gave offence. The Prologue of this play gives an indication of what audiences were expecting: Day says that they demand bawdy, topical satire and rich poetry. These, Day says, cannot all be put into one play, but he does introduce a great deal of bawdiness and satire. In the satire he points at King James himself and his well-known predilection for favourites. This caused offence and Day and the other men responsible were imprisoned in the Bridewell.

Around this date the company seems to have become autonomous. It no longer had the queen's patronage and a London goldsmith, Robert Keyser, became financially responsible for it. Keyser changed the name to the Children of the Blackfriars and at first, under his regime, the company was successful financially and kept out of trouble with the authorities. But in 1608 the theatres were closed by the king because two plays were considered subversive. One play has disappeared, but contemporary reports suggest that it contained an attack on the king. The other, George Chapman's *Conspiracy and Tragedy of Byron* (1608), dealt, as the title suggests, with a conspiracy against a king.

Marston, too, was summoned before the Privy Council and committed to Newgate in 1608 for some offence which is now not known and, thereafter, he ceased his association with the Children of Blackfriars. James, though, relented and the company was playing again in 1609 when the children appeared at court. The company then left Blackfriars and appeared at Whitefriars. It was under this name that it performed for the king five times in the winter of 1609/10 and was then allowed to assume the title of the Children of the Queen's Revels once again. The letters patent which decreed this named five men, Robert Daborne, Phillippe Rosseter, John Tarbock, Richard Iones and Robert Browne, who were 'From tyme to tyme to provide keepe and bring vpp a convenient number of children, and them to practise and exercise in the quality of playing.' No mention of any financial arrangements was made – it seems the boys were making enough money to support themselves. Browne and Iones were professional actors who had, presumably, retired.

Ben Jonson's play written for the children and called *Epicene or The Silent Woman* (1609/10) was a great success, though it was for a short time banned, as Lady Arabella Stuart, a cousin of the king, thought that it made an unpleasant comment on her engagement to a shifty continental prince. Performed at Whitefriars, the play deals with tranvestism and stretches the subject to the extreme. In it Morose, a crusty old bachelor, decides to marry so as to disinherit his nephew and heir, Sir Dauphine Eugenie. But, as he is averse to noise, he wants a woman who will remain silent. His barber introduces him to Epicene, who though silent during the courtship, when married never stops talking! To aggravate the situation Dauphine and his friends, Truewit and Clerimont, arrive with other gallants and musicians to celebrate the nuptials. Among the uninvited guests are the Collegiate Ladies, a society of women who live apart from their husbands but entertain all the wits and gallants of the town. Other noisy characters invade the scene until Morose, almost driven mad by the noise, consents to give Dauphine £500 a year and a reversion of his property. Dauphine snatches off Epicene's wig, revealing a boy whom he has trained for the part. This is a heartless play, but it reveals much of the money-grabbing and sexual ambiguity in Jacobean society. *Epicene* remained popular: it was the first play to be revived when the theatres reopened with the Restoration in 1660 and Samuel Pepys thought highly of it, saying that it was 'the best comedy, I think, that ever was wrote'. Playing Epicene was Edmund Kynaston.

Marston's unfinished play *The Insatiate Countess*, was completed by William Barksted and published in 1613. It is typical of the dark sexual plays of the decade, similar in atmosphere to John Webster's more popular works. It is amoral, the protagonist sleeping with one man after another, and her lust inevitably causing murder. The part of the Countess is intriguing because she uses her power and sex appeal to gain what she wants. The sub-plot, which has a comic side to it, treats of two husbands of citizen rank who are insanely suspicious of their wives, and the play encompasses not one, but two bed-tricks. The husbands, by now demented with jealousy and anger, admit to a murder they did not commit. However, all comes well in the end. The two plots – one tragic, one comic – sit uneasily together but the play illustrates, as

G.K. Hunter says in his book on English drama of the period 'Social and personal, honour and love, are still opposites but no longer sharply incompatible.'

In 1615 Robert Iones and Philip Kingman, together with Rosseter and Reeve, were licensed to build a new playhouse in Porter's Hall. The only play recorded as having been given there by the Children is by Beaumont and Fletcher and is called *The Scornful Lady*. In 1615, the chief actor of the company, Nathan Field joined the King's Men and the Children of the Queen's Revels seem to have stopped performing in London, though there are records of them touring up until 1617.

The Children of the Revels and the Children of St Paul's were the two professional boys' companies in London. Although the St Paul's boys were funded, the Children of the Revels seem to have been self-supporting and relied entirely on their box office. Audiences that went to see the Children and paid a sixpence entrance fee, were, in the main, the upper classes and the young men from the Inns of Court. Sixpence would have been a considerable sum of money for anyone whose annual wage was around £5, which is what a skilled craftsman could expect to earn. This sophisticated audience must have influenced the type of plays performed. Lyly's works, which relied heavily on rhetoric and classical settings, would have appealed to those who had studied the classics at universities, but the later plays, those performed after the closure of the theatres and in the new reign of James, have a distinctly gamey feel. Sexually explicit, exceptionally so for the times, with bawdy jokes and lines, and with amoral behaviour, they reflect the more raffish nature of the Stuart court. The subject matter dealt with in all theatres had now changed to include corruption, sexual freedom and an emphasis of the darker side of a woman's life. There must, too, have been an added pleasure for some in seeing young boys act such decadent parts when, perhaps, they had only a partial understanding of the real meaning.

Although these companies were professional and playing in London, there were other troupes and schools. The Chapel Royal at Windsor gave entertainments at court during Elizabeth's reign, and E.K. Chambers conjectures that boys from the chapel may have taken parts as the children in *The Merry Wives of Windsor*, but that, though pleasing, is mere fantasy. Westminster School also presented plays, as did Eton College, St Paul's Grammar School, Westminster Grammar School and the Westminster choirboys. At the Merchant Taylors School the enlightened schoolmaster Richard Mulcaster encouraged his boys in rhetoric and acting, and they gave public performances in the Common Hall of the Merchant Taylors Guild to a paying audience. The Merchant Taylors stopped public performances there, but the boys continued to act and sometimes appeared at court. Sir James Whitelocke, who became a judge, wrote of his schooldays: 'I was brought up at school under Mr Mulcaster, in the famous school of the Merchantaylors in London. . . . Yeerly he presented playes to the court, in which his scholars were the only actors, and I among them, and by that means taughte them good behaviour and audacitye.'

Whatever the quality of the boys' acting, and it must have been excellent to attract a sophisticated audience for so many years, the opportunities that it presented to playwrights were enormous. Many Elizabethan dramatists wrote for the boys' companies. And although many of their plays are lost, those extant are among the best of the period. Some are still performed, others ought to be, not only as a curiosity, but because they are good plays. The boys' companies may have been only a fashion, but the work that they did was notable and though it remains a curiosity, it was surely a unique and important piece of theatrical history.

CHAPTER NINE

Boys will be Girls and Girls will be Boys

'the glass of fashion and the mould of form'

One of the Puritans' objections to boy players was that they wore women's clothes. They quoted a passage from Deuteronomy: 22:5, which says: 'A woman shall not wear that which pertainth unto a man, neither shall a man put on a woman's garment.' But, this passage does not define which garments pertain to which sex! In the ancient, civilised world everyone wore skirts and, because of the Commandment prohibiting the representation of living things, we have no pictorial records of what the Jews who wrote this edict wore. St Paul exhorts women to cover their heads, but he does not define what were women's garments and what were men's. In the Roman culture in which he lived and of which he claimed citizenship men wore short tunics with togas while women wore long, flowing dresses. It was the barbarians whose men wore breeches, and who made the distinction between men and women's clothes. The medieval church defined this distinction and this was underlined by the cult of the Virgin Mary who was, and is, held up as a paradigm to all Roman Catholic women. Portraits always show her modestly dressed in a long skirt and with a veil on her head. But historical accuracy was not a preoccupation and the image of the Virgin is that of the medieval and Renaissance painters and sculptors. It was a grave breach of good behaviour for a woman to wear anything other than a long dress. So entrenched was this edict that one of the charges against Joan of Arc was that she wore men's clothes.

In times of social unrest, though, women don men's clothes, or a version of them. After the French Revolution, for example, women, for the first time, wore   jackets and great coats cut after the style of men's military uniforms. After the First World War women cut their hair and shortened their skirts, and in the Second World War women wore trousers for certain types of work. After that war trousers became acceptable for work and for casual wear. It was not until the contraceptive pill became widely available that women wore trouser suits formally and now, even women barristers are allowed to wear them in court and, Margaret Beckett, Leader of the House of Commons, has worn them at the Opening of the Houses of Parliament.

In Elizabeth's day a great social change took place. The church in England was becoming the Church of England and the cult of the Virgin Mary had disappeared, along with the statues of her in church. She became idolatrous. In her place Elizabeth became Gloriana, an image the queen herself cherished and preserved carefully, as Dr Roy Strong has shown in his *Portraits of Queen Elizabeth I*. One of the manifestations of this change was that women started to wear men's clothes. There is no record of Elizabeth herself wearing them, and among the 190 items listed by Janet Arnold in *Queen Elizabeth's Wardrobe Unlock'd*, no breeches are mentioned, though obviously the Royal Wardrobe's tailors would have made them for courtiers and servants. It would be splendid to think that the queen wore breeches when she rode, but there is no evidence for it. But the *elegantes* of her day and those of her successor did don doublet and hose. In poetry, pamphlets and plays we find descriptions of women in what were considered men's clothes and much of Elizabethan dress was worn by both men and women.

The doublet was common to both sexes as we have seen (plates 8, 16, 17, 18) and examples for the aristocracy and the emerging merchant class were very decorative. Over it could be worn, by both sexes, a sleeveless jerkin. Hats, too, were common to both sexes. The high beaver hat, or coptain, shown in a miniature by Isaac Oliver (plate 17) of a young woman, is the same as that worn by the Brothers Browne (plate 16), also by Oliver, as is the wide collar. Ruffs, bonnets, collars and gloves were all garments worn by both sexes. The smock was the main undergarment. Generally made in linen it was of the same design for both men and women, though rich people's smocks would be embroidered at neck and sleeve. In Ben Jonson's *Every Man in his Humour* there is a scene where a man wears a woman's smock while she washes his and this is done without any comment. The smock was worn in bed: a nightgown was a version of the old medieval gown (similar to a university gown of today) and was sometimes still worn by elderly people for day wear, as is seen in a portrait of Lord Burghley in the National Portrait Gallery.

The general effect of costumes was of richness, as they were heavily embroidered and made of exquisite fabrics – velvet, sarcenet, damask and taffeta. George Gascoigne wrote:

But when his bonnet, buttoned with gold,
His comely cape, begarded all with gay,
His bombast hose, with linings manifold
His knot silk socks and all his quaint array.

And in 'Elegie XIX (Going to Bed)' John Donne refers to a 'spangled breastplate', a 'busk', and a 'wyerie Coronet'.

It was the donning of breeches, swords and daggers together with plumed, broad-brimmed hats which caused the greatest offence and prompted the fiercest invective. Letter writer and scholar John Chamberlain wrote on 25 January 1620:

> Yesterday the bishop of London called together all his Clergie about this towne, and told them he had expressed commaundment from the King to will them to inveigh vehemently and bitterly in theyre sermons against the insolencie of our women, and theyre wearing of brode brimd hats, pointed doublets, theyre hair cut short or shorne, and some of them stillettaes or poniards, and other such trinkekects of like moment; adding withal that yf pulpit admonitions will not reforme them he wold proceed by another course; the truth is the world is very far out of order, but whether this will men yt God knows.

A year previously, a cleric, John Williams, had forestalled his bishop by publishing *A Sermon of Apparell* in which he declared that while God had created man and woman separately, now 'the deuill hath ioyn'd them, that, is now become *mulier monstrosa superne*, half man halfe woman' and that when a woman attended church she caused a distraction when she appeared in man's attire:

> What flesh and blood hath his thoughts so staunch, but must be distracted in his Church devotions, at the *prodigious* apparition of our *women?* . . . For a woman therefore to come into Churche . . . halfe male, and halfe female . . . lifting vp towards his throne *two plaister'd eies and a polled head* . . . In *Sattin* (I warrant *you*) in stead of sackecloth . . . standing most manly vpon her *points*, by wagging a *Feather* to defie the *World*, and carrying a *dagger* . . . to enter God's house, as if it were a Playhouse.

Thomas Adams, talking about what he observed in London, wrote:

. . . both he and shee. For if they had no more euident distinction of sexe, then they have to shape, they would be all man, or rather all woman: for the *Amazons* beare away the Bell . . . *Hic Mulier* will shortly be good latine, if tis transmigration hold; for whither on horsebacke, or on foot, there is no difference.

'*Hic Mulier*' became a well-known epithet for women in men's clothes for in February 1620 a pamphlet *Hic Mulier: or the Man-Woman: Being a Medecine to cure the Coltish Disease of the Staggers in the Masculine-Feminines of our Times* was published anonymously. The title page shows one woman waiting to have her hair cut, while her companion tries on a broad-brimmed, plumed hat. Both wear skirts with doublets. The whole pamphlet fulminates not only against women wearing masculine dress, but against the increasingly aggressive behaviour of men and says that this fashion extends itself not only to the rich, but is rife among the burghers and citizens as well. According to this author, women not only wore the doublet but left it open to show their breasts. Furthermore, the wearing of daggers, swords and poniards also upset the writer. Although he does mention women wearing breeches this seems to concern him less than the wearing of weapons:

Cloudy Ruffianly broad-brimm'd Hatte, and wanton Feather . . . the loose, lasciuous . . . embracement of a French doublet . . . most ruffianly short lockes. . . . for Needles, Swords . . . for Prayer bookes, bawdy ligs is not halfe man, halfe woman . . . but all Odyous, all Divell.

This pamphlet was soon followed by *Haec Vir; or, The Womanish-Man: Being an Answere to the late Books intituled Hic-Mulier. Exprest in a briefe Dialogue between Haec-Vir the Womanish Man, and Hic-Mulier the Man-Woman.* In this essay it is the man who is accused of being womanish, thus making women respond to this fault by becoming more dominant and wearing men's clothes.

The controversy, though, had been discussed since the 1570s when George Gascoigne wrote of women:

> What be they? women? Masking in men's weedes?
> With dutchin dublets, and jerkins iaggde?
> With high copt hates, and fethers flaunt a flaunt?
> They be so sure even *Wo* to *Men* in dede.
>   ['The Steele Glass; (1576), *English Reprints*, vol. 5 pp. 82–3)

Philip Stubbes in *Anatomy of Abuses* (1583) wrote: 'dublets and Jerkins as men have heer, buttoned up the brest, and made with wings, welts, and pinions on the shoulder points', Men were castigated for their dress also, and this blurred the difference between the sexes even more. William Prynne writing in *Histrio-Mastix, the Player's Scourge or Actor's Tragedy*, 1632, asks angrily:

> For whence is it that many of our gentry lately degenerated into a more than Sardanapalian effeminacy; that they are now so fantastic in their apparel, so womanish in their frizzled periwigs, love-locks, and long effeminate powdered pounced hair; so mimical in their gestures; so effeminate in their lives, so player-like in their deportment, so amorous in their embracements . . . is it not principally from their resort to plays, to masques, and such-like antic, apish pastimes . . .

Special invective was reserved for the players. Dr Rainoldes, a leading Oxford divine, wrote in *The Overthrow of Stage-Playes* (1599): 'The apparel of women [on boys] is a great provocation of men to lust and lecherie' and further 'A womans garment being put on a man doth vehemently touch and move hime with the remembrance and imagination of a woman; and the imagination of a thing desirable doth stir up desire.'

Thomas Randle's poem 'On a maide of honour seene by a scholar in Somerset Garden' shows the confusion that was occasioned by cross-dressing:

As once in lacke I disrespected walkt
Where glittering courtiers in their Tissues stalkt
I cast by chaunce my melancholy eye
Upon a woman (as I thought) past by.
But when I viewed her ruffe, and beaver reard
As if *Priapus*-like she would have feard
The ravenous *Harpies* from their clustered grapes,
Then I began much to mistrust her shape;
When viewing curiously, away she slipt,
And in the fount her whited hand she dipt,
The angry water as if wrong'd thereby,
Ranne murmuring thence a second touch to fly,
At which she stalkes, and as she goes,
She views the situation of each rose;
And having higher ray'sd her gowne, she gaz'd
Upon her crimson stockings which amaz'd
Blusht at her open impudence, and sent
Reflection to her cheeke, for punishment.
And thus I stood the Gardiner chaunce to passe,
My friend (quoth I) what is this stately lasse?
A maid of honour Sir, said he, and goes
Leaving a riddle, was enough to pose
The crafty *Oedipus* for I could see
Nor mayde, nor honour, sure noe modesty.

Certainly when looking at the portraits and miniatures of the day it is often difficult to see who is male and who is female. The Unknown Woman in plate 17 is one of several androgynous portraits, while the Unknown Young Man in plate 18, painted by Nicholas Hilliard in his yellow doublet, ruff and black bonnet might easily be a woman, as could the young man in plate 19. A miniature of Ludwig Philip in the Victoria and Albert Museum again portrays a man who can hardly be described as overtly masculine. All these could pass as portraits of either men or women. The man/woman, master/mistress was prevalent and accepted as part of life, except by the more hysterical and puritan element in society.

There has been discussion among scholars about the extent to which the Elizabethan theatre was homoerotic. The argument that it was so, is based on the patriarchal nature of Elizabethan and Jacobean society, which limited the scope of women and did not allow them to appear on the stage. It was considered a disgrace for a woman to make herself conspicuous in public. So, the argument runs, as the boys had to play women's parts the theatre became a place for homoerotic emotions, a place where they were rampant. That there was considerable writing on the subject, that some men felt uneasy about seeing boys wear women's clothing in public, is obvious. In the widest sense of the word, the boys were transvestites, but by necessity and not through any genetic disposition or wilful defiance of the social code. John Rainoldes' castigation, quoted above, and a further statement that the wearing of women's clothes by the boy players was an 'occasion of wantonness and lust' can be read as a protest about homoerotic feelings, but equally as a protest against any sort of eroticism. If it is read as being against homosexuality in the theatre, then it says as much against Rainoldes' homophobic fears as about the actuality of what was seen in the theatre. Rainoldes equates the theatre with prostitution, too, but he always has a fine line in hysteria concerning a society where cross-dressing and unisex dressing were accepted.

Like our own time, this was an age that explored sexual ambiguity, as can be seen in a great deal of its literature, not only in that written for the stage. Doubtless there were paedophiliac and homosexual men and women in the audience who went to the theatre to be titillated, for the theatre deals with the erotic, and cross-dressing can be part of the erotic. Heterosexual members of the audience take this as part of the entertainment and are not affected by it. The Elizabethan theatre did not offer sex objects for heterosexual men, though the audience seems to have provided them, if some of the poets are to be believed. Work done by Alan Bray and Alan Macfarlane on court records of Assizes and Sessions shows a paucity of indictments for sodomy, the only indictable homosexual offence (four in Essex, for example, between December 1612 and March 1618, and similar numbers for other counties). This seems to suggest that the polemicists were aiming at a small target. There was also a railing against 'effeminate' behaviour, but in the sixteenth and seventeenth centuries this word could also be used for a man who was a great lover of women. John Donne, for example, described himself as effeminate 'because I love women's joy'. Today, it is estimated that about 10 per cent of the population is homosexual and there is no reason to believe that there was a higher proportion of homosexuals in Elizabethan England than today, though sexual divisions were not so defined as they are in our more prurient age. Indeed, the word homosexual did not exist in the sixteenth and seventeenth centuries. That androgyny existed and was exploited by writers is certain.

The playwrights, Shakespeare above all, write about androgyny and this must have been helpful to the boy players. There are many *double entendres* in the plays but they are well in character, and, indeed, help to reveal character. And, somehow, much of the salacious talk becomes funnier if said innocently. Desdemona and Iago on the quayside indulge in witty, sexy talk, but it is entirely in character – Desdemona, after all, is on her honeymoon – and it adds to the febrile atmosphere of the scene. In *All's Well That Ends Well*, Helena, another independent woman, who is a doctor's daughter, also speaks frankly and sexily, but this, again, reveals her upfront character. Feminist critics often express the view that Shakespeare (and other dramatists) 'degraded' women, taking *The Taming of the Shrew* and in *Cymbeline* Posthumus's speech beginning 'It is a woman's part' as evidence. But this is to impute to Shakespeare, himself, what his characters express. That he was aware of and could express the hatred that men can feel against women who have, or whom they think have, betrayed them is part of his ability as a great dramatist with an exceptional knowledge of human nature. To attempt to deduce from his characters what Shakespeare actually thought about androgyny and cross-dressing is a fruitless task. He exploited the fashions of his day, as did other dramatists, in order to help the boy players. Shakespeare especially exploited the woman/man confusion throughout his career: from Julia in *Two Gentlemen of Verona*, to the three women in the *Merchant of Venice*, with Rosalind in *As You Like It*, and Viola in *Twelfth Night*, through to one of the late plays, *Cymbeline*, where the Princess Innogen appears not only in a boy's costume but also dressed as a citizen. Today, directors sometimes extend the wearing of men's clothes. Jonathan Miller in the 1984 Old Vic production of *The Tempest* had his Miranda (Rudi Davies) wear Prospero's shirt and breeches. Stephen Unwin dressed Hippolyta in breeches (the Century Touring Company's production of *A Midsummer Night's Dream*, 1993), while in 1979, Ronald Eyre's Desdemona (Suzanne

Bertish) in the Royal Shakespeare Company's *Othello* arrived in Cyprus in men's clothing; and in Philip Prowse's National Theatre production of *The Duchess of Malfi* (1985), Sheila Hancock as the Cardinal's Mistress also wore breeches. Dekker and Middleton exploited the whole man/woman convention in *The Roaring Girl*.

We know how Shakespeare liked his boy players to be dressed as men from reading *The Two Gentlemen of Verona* (*c*. 1588), Act 2 scene vii:

Julia	. . . Gentle Lucetta, fit me with such weeds As may beseem some well-reputed page.
Lucetta	Why then your ladyship must cut her hair.
Julia	No, girl, I'll knit it up in silken strings With twenty odd conceited true-love knots To be fantastic may become a youth Of greater time than I shall show to be.
Lucetta	What fashion, madam, shall I make your breeches?
Julia	That fits as well as 'Tell me, my good lord, What compass will you wear your farthingale?' Why, e'en what fashion thou best likes, Lucetta.
Lucetta	You must needs have a cod-piece, madam.
Julia	Out, out, Lucetta. That will be ill-favoured.
Lucetta	A round hose, madam, now that's not worth a pin Unless you have a cod-piece to stick pins on.

Julia   Lucetta, as thou lov'st me let me have
           What thou dost think'st meet and is most mannerly . . .

In *The Roaring Girl* (1611), based on a real woman called Moll Frith who was noted for wearing men's clothes, there is a scene where the heroine, called Moll Cutpurse in the play, discusses her garments with a tailor (Act 2 scene ii). It is obvious that she is ordering breeches and decides to have a pair in a fashion called Dutch slops (plate 13) which will take a yard of material more, and will 'stand out round and full'. She had complained that the previous pair she had was somewhat 'stiff between the legs' and the Tailor reassures her that this pair will be 'open enough'. Another character, Sir Alexander, grumbles that: 'I have bought up my son to marry a Dutch slop and a French Doublet, a cod-piece daughter' (Act 2 scene ii).

The costume of the day – the padded doublet, ruffs and collars – and the style of hats, were helpful to the boy players. Padded doublets, if done up, made the same shape for both men and women. Even the underclothes would help to disguise a boy. The smock, worn by both sexes was a starched garment, so when Desdemona, for example, undresses, the smock would fall to the ankles in an inverted V-shape, revealing nothing.

What then did the Elizabethans actually see when they went to the playhouse? Their expectations of and responses to the players would be totally different from those of a modern audience who are more visually orientated than those of the Elizabethan age. The magnificent language was paramount then, not only for revealing character and furthering the plot, but also for describing the scene. They expected to be dazzled by the ear and the training in schools, where lessons were by rote and emphasis was put on good speech, made the audiences more receptive to language. Today, what we see in the theatre is as important as what we hear.

Views on feminine attractiveness were also different from today's expectations of slimness, long legs and a good bosom. The doublet was a concealing garment, as was most Elizabethan clothing with the exception of round hose – those puffed up breeches that showed a great deal of leg! A farthingale would hide the boys' male characteristics and a doublet disguise his lack of feminine ones. Audiences and actors, of course, collude in a performance. The audience is aware of itself as an audience and of acting collectively as an audience, and each individual member of an audience is also aware of being himself and has his own reasons for being in that audience. As part of an audience he becomes bigger than himself, catching fire (or boredom) from his fellow members, experiencing deeper emotions than he would if he were alone. Most members of a present-day audience have had the experience when watching a film in a cinema of laughing (or weeping) copiously; but when they see that film again on television or video, sitting alone, although the emotion of joy or sadness is felt, it is not overtly expressed. In the theatre the audience has a duty to respond. Actors talk about 'a good house' – one which has responded to all the points the actors wished to make. A 'bad house' has made the wrong response or no response at all. Actors, therefore, need our collusion. In *The Psychology of the Imagination*, Jean-Paul Sartre describes what he sees when watching the music-hall artiste, Franconay, doing an impersonation of Maurice Chevalier. Sartre recognises the imitation, realising that Franconay has produced an image of Chevalier. He compares the two and the audience compares the two, using their recollections of Chevalier to do so. As Sartre writes:

A consciousness is through and through a synthesis, completely withdrawn into itself: it is only at the very heart of this internal synthesis that it can join itself to another proceeding or succeeding consciousness by an act of retention or protention. Moreover, if one consciousness is to act on another, it must be retained and recreated by the consciousness on which it is to act. There are no passivities, but internal assimilations and disintegrations at the very heart of an intentional synthesis, which is transparent to itself. One consciousness is not the cause of another: it motivates it.

So, when an audience watches, it is constantly aware of both the person (in this case Franconay) *and* the person she is imitating (Maurice Chevalier). But Franconay can never *be* Chevalier – she is female, she has not his body, his voice, his unique presence. She is both herself and Chevalier, both *personae* being obvious to the audience, but she is also her other self, aware of what she is doing. She is using her imagination to re-create in her audience's collective mind its own recollections of Chevalier.

But Franconay was doing an imitation of a well-known entertainer. An actor does something different. He is creating an imaginary character and, in the case of Elizabethan drama, a character of which the first audiences knew nothing, for they had no way of reading the text beforehand as we can today. The experience of seeing a new play is totally different from seeing a play with which one is familiar and about which one can say 'That was not my idea of Hamlet', for example. The audience of a new play has no preconception of what the actor is trying to portray. Although costume can, and in Elizabethan times did, reveal a character's class, profession or trade and a particular actor might be known for playing a particular 'line', the audience has no idea of the attributes of the character until the play unfolds. An Elizabethan audience would be full of expectation about character and plot, would not be distracted by visual complexity, and would be aware of itself as both audience and as a collection of individuals watching a play in which actors were telling a story with characters who were both part of their consciousness and the consciousness of the dramatist. The players were also aware of what they were doing, responding to the audience's reaction and editing their performances to suit that audience. This makes for a complex and multi-layered experience.

So our cross-dressing boy player was taking part in something that was mainly happening in the minds of people, who had come to the theatre to be entertained and were willing to do their part by entering into a collusion that what they were seeing was real. There were few effects to distract and alienate; there were only words and costume and acting. The audience and the actors all decided to see something that was a real woman, though on another level they were well aware that 'she' was a cross-dressed boy, much as a present-day audience conspires with the soprano playing Oktavian in *Der Rosenkavalier* that he is a boy who then pretends to be a girl, as does also the singer of Cherubino in *The Marriage of Figaro*.

But something else is also happening. The actors and audience are also colluding with the writer, to believe in his vision and, thus, to make something greater than what is actually on the page. The philosopher Ludwig Wittgenstein expressed this about music. He pointed out in a lecture at Cambridge, in about 1930, that:

. . . the relation between a musical score and a performance cannot be grasped casually (as though we find mysteriously, that a certain score *causes* us to play in a certain way), nor can the rules that connect the two be exhaustively described – for, given a certain interpretation, *any* playing can be made to accord with the score. Eventually, we just have to 'see the rule in the relation between playing and score'. If we cannot see it, no amount of explanation is going to make it comprehensible; if we can see, there comes a point at which explanations are superfluous – we do not need any kind of 'fundamental' explanation.

To apply this to the Elizabethan theatre, it can be said that the audience and the boy players, colluding in what was 'belief' and having superb words to appreciate and help, were agreeing with each other that the 'fundamental' explanation (to use Wittgenstein's words) was superfluous, and what they were doing and watching transcended any mundane reality, producing a greater truth about which there are no logical explanations.

But the boy's body was present, and identity is very much tied up with physical attributes. Could a boy really convincingly portray a woman? What did the Elizabethans think about sexuality? In today's prurient society people are labelled by their sexuality – heterosexual, homosexual and bisexual. These terms meant nothing to the Elizabethans. Men could, and did, have passionate friendships that might or might not be sexually expressed. Hamlet's speech to Horatio is a fictional representation of this type of friendship, but the relationship is not overtly sexual. Some of Shakespeare's sonnets show an ambiguity about sex, and the young men and young women in the plays show great affection one to the other. The sleeping arrangements of even the very rich (corridors had not been invented and bedrooms led out of each other) made bodies very familiar and less an object of salacious enquiry than now. As we have seen, clothes minimised sexual differences too. The cult of women wearing men's clothes and men becoming 'effeminate' was prevalent throughout the period, and so the sexual differences were blurred. The boy player, portraying a girl who was wearing men's clothes, would be more believable to an age used to women wearing men's clothes. Nowadays it is sometimes difficult to tell young women from young men when they are both wearing jeans, T-shirts, trainers and hair which can be either long or short. So the sexual differences in the Elizabethan age were similarly indistinct. The master/mistress figure of the boy player would be entirely credible. There would be no doubt in the audience's mind that this was a girl being portrayed on the stage, a reality of the imagination – a different experience, and one entered into willingly from seeing a real girl, just as King Lear or Hamlet are not living beings but products of Shakespeare's imagination and the acting of Richard Burbage. The truth of the imagination is what theatre deals in and when entering its doors this is what an audience consents to conspire in.

Conclusion

In 1611, Thomas Coryate, after a visit to Italy, wrote in *Crudeties*: 'I saw women acte, a thing I never saw before . . . and they performed it with as good grace, action, gesture and whatsoever convenient for a Player, as ever I saw any masculine Actor.' This compliment to the Italian actresses underlines the excellence of English actors, boys included. That the boys were successful is obvious. A society that enjoyed going to the theatre (6,000 people out of a population of *c.* 300,000 could have gone every day when the theatres were open), that had high standards of speech and singing, would not have tolerated bad acting. Although there is little comment on acting at all in contemporary literature (drama critics not yet being invented), what does appear is complimentary. That boys could deceive by their appearances is shown by the poem on page 181 and polemics concerning the evil of their appearing at all seem to indicate that they were a force to be reckoned with. There are one or two references that praise a boy's acting. Henry Jackson of Corpus Christi College, Oxford, saw the King's Men play *Othello* in 1610. In a letter he wrote:

At vero Desdemona illa apud nos a marito occisa, quanquam optime semper causam egit, interfecta tamen magis movebat; cum in facto in leto decumbens spectantium misericordiam ipso vultu imploret. [In truth, that famous Desdemona who was killed in front of us by her husband, acted her whole part supremely well, but surpassed herself when she was actually killed, being yet more moving, for when she fell back upon the bed she implored pity from the spectators by her very face – *author's translation.*]

Although Jackson does not mention the age of the boy, it is obvious that he was moved by his excellent acting and thoroughly convinced – he refers to the actor as 'her' continually throughout.

Another testimony to the boys' abilities is that of Thomas Platter, who came from Switzerland. He saw *Julius Caesar* in 1599 and commented on the actors' skills: '. . . at the end of the comedy, they danced as was their custom very elegantly: two people in men's clothes and two in women's, combining wonderfully with each other'.

Thomas Heywood in *An Apology for Actors* (1608), while seeming not entirely to approve of boy actors, nonetheless pays an unstated compliment to their ability: 'To see our youths attired in the habit of women, who knows not what their intents be? Who cannot distinguish them by their names, assuredly knowing that they are but to represent such a lady, at such a time appointed?'

None of these comments disparages the actors; all observers have been impressed by their skills. Today, it might seem odd that such a convention should be tolerated, but the Elizabethan theatre and audiences accepted it and worked within it. The women's parts are, when looked at from the point of view of the boys who played them, not necessarily the psychologically rounded women that it is assumed today that they should be. Peter Brook in *The Empty Space* tells of an experience he had of giving Goneril's speech 'Sir, I love you' to someone who had never read *King Lear*:

She read it very simply – the speech itself emerged full of eloquence and charm. I then explained to her that it was supposed to be the speech of a wicked woman and suggested her reading every word for hypocrisy. She tried to do so, and the audience saw what a hard unnatural wrestling with the simple music of the words was involved when she sought to act to a definition. . . . The words are those of a lady of style and breeding accustomed to expressing herself in public, someone with ease and social aplomb. As for clues to her character, only the façade is presented and this, we see, is eloquent and attractive.

What Brook is saying here is that actors should forget the critical encrustations that the parts have accrued, and try to read the parts as if they were new-minted as, indeed, the creators of the roles had to do. Then it is found that the way the parts are written technically, the rather simple but strong emotions that they express, are within the capabilities of an imaginative boy who was also a fully trained professional. As well, to help them the boys had the wonderful flexible medium of the iambic pentameter or very rhythmical prose. This helped them to express emotion. As Peter Hall points out in *Making an Exhibition of Myself*: 'Shakespeare constantly heightens emotions by creating irregularities in the verse. He writes against the verse, yet always preserves it. It is about to break and never quite does. . . . Out of these breathtaking irregularities, the actor can express extreme feeling.'

As has been shown throughout this book the boys were very skilled in the arts that comprise a good performance, and what scant evidence there is praises them: the simple speech, characterisation that was within the knowledge of a boy makes the women's parts different in construction to the men's parts. So why then did the boys cease to be part of our theatrical tradition?

In James I's reign, and even more under Charles I, the masque became the most favoured court entertainment. Companies of the

South Bank were aware of this and plays themselves had in them elements of the masque. For example, *The Tempest* (1611) has a masque within it; in *All is True* (*Henry VIII*) (1613) the King and his friends dress as masquers and Katherine has a vision; *The Winter's Tale* has a pastoral scene. But, above all, women took part in masques. Aristocratic ladies, including the two queens Anne of Denmark and Henrietta Maria, participated in these entertainments and proved that women could act without sacrificing their traditional female role. It is also interesting that the word 'actress' was used for the first time about Queen Henrietta Maria when she appeared in a masque on Shrove Tuesday 1626. The richer element of the audience now became used to seeing women act. However, this movement did not extend to the professional stage. It was other events that caused the downfall of the boy player. The English Civil War had the greatest effect on the theatre.

The theatres stood empty during the greater part of the war, some of the actors actually involved in it. The Puritans, who won, suppressed the theatre entirely, an edict in 1647 declaring that actors were '. . . incorrigible and vicious offenders who will now be compelled by whip, and stocks, and gives, and prison fare, to obey ordinances which hitherto they have treated with contempt.' The House of Commons was determined to crush harlotry play-acting. Those that tried to circumnavigate the decree were attacked by Puritan soldiers and theatres were destroyed. There were some brave members of the aristocracy who held private performances in their houses, Holland House being one such venue. There was some touring as well, William Davenant – who claimed to be Shakespeare's illegitimate son and had a company – was imprisoned, and only saved from execution by the intervention of the poet, John Milton. Davenant produced entertainments towards the end of the Puritan reign, one of them having the cumbersome title of *The Cruelty of the Spaniards in Peru, exprest by instrumental and vocal music, and by the art of perspective in Scenes.* The diarist John Evelyn described it as a musical entertainment much inferior to Italian opera, and seems to have been bored by it. Players, though, were living through dangerous times. Cromwell disliked the plays of Shakespeare and the theatre generally. After his death in 1658, conditions eased somewhat, but the theatres on the South Bank had been destroyed or dismantled, providing materials for housing.

It was not until 1660 that the players had hope again. That year Charles II claimed his throne and the puritanical past began to fade. During the Commonwealth Charles had spent his time in France at the court of his cousin, Louis XIV. The splendid Sun King was an accomplished dancer in his youth, who performed in lavish and magnificent masques. Charles also saw performances of the plays of Molière, who employed women as actresses. Charles, though impoverished, was witness to splendour and excellence in acting and drama. He enjoyed the theatre and during his reign it prospered. One of his first acts as king was to give royal patents for two companies – one, to Davenant and his Duke's Servants, the other to Thomas Killigrew and his partner Herbert, who eventually settled in Drury Lane and formed the King's Company. Killigrew's company appeared in a tennis court, until his theatre was ready.

But what of the women's parts, who were to play them? It was more than thirteen years since there had been regular companies in which the boys could learn their skills with experienced actors. Even the youngest boy apprentice then was now past puberty and, assuredly, had a broken voice. As a pamphlet of 1643 had lamented: 'our boyes, ere we shall have the libertie to acte againe, will be grown out of use like crackt organ pipes, and have faces as old as our flags.' There is some evidence to suggest that for the first years of Charles's reign, women's parts were played by young men using falsetto voices. Three of them, including Charles Hart who later was much praised for his Othello, were employed by Killigrew, and seemed to please the audiences, but they were obviously men. Another actor, Edward Kynaston, achieved great success; Samuel Pepys, no mean authority, said that he was 'the loveliest lady' that he had ever seen. Kynaston, still in costume, used to go off to Hyde Park with 'ladies of quality' after the performances. Although he continued acting for many years in male parts after he became too old to play women, using falsetto had affected his voice badly and he spoke with a very disagreeable tone. Kynaston's looks remained and after his death his obituary declared that: 'it is indisputable among the judicious whether any woman that succeeded him so sensibly touched the audience as he'.

The king, probably because he had seen actresses in France, soon issued a royal charter which said:

> And wee doe likewise permit and give leave that all the women's part to be acted in either of the two said companies for the time to come may be performed by women soe long as their recreacones, which by reason of the abuse aforesaid were scandalous and offensive, may by such reformation be esteemed not onely harmless delight, but useful and instructive representations of human life, to such of our good subjects as shall resort to the same.

The 'abuse foresaid' being, of course, the impersonation of women by men. Charles was ever adept at turning a situation to his own advantage and by agreeing with the Puritans that cross-dressing was lewd, he managed to have what he wished – women playing on the stage. Mistress Margaret Hughes appeared on Saturday 8 December 1660 in the tennis court that Killigrew was using and so had the distinction of being the first professional English actress.

Though the actresses were welcome, young men still appeared. However, they gradually faded out. Also, a change in the way women were regarded had some influence on the theatre. In the Restoration period women were seen in a more enlightened fashion: they were regarded as having some individuality and not required to be as subservient as they had been. Their remarkable record of bravery during the war received recognition. The theatre audience had changed too. It was more connected with the court, in that courtiers and the king went to the public theatres instead of commanding performances at court as Elizabeth and James I had done.

There are people who do not believe that boys could play the parts written by the Elizabethan dramatists, but today the roles come with an accretion of ideas and traditions passed on by actresses through many generations. We look at the parts from a different point of view to their first players and first audiences. We have more complicated ideas about the plays, conventions that have grown up around them. We, too, have a different custom of presentation. Although we no longer cut the plays drastically to make way for scenic effects (for example Irving's production of *Romeo and Juliet* in 1882 had three changes of scenery in the last scene of the play) and, generally, especially in the small-space theatres, have simpler scenery, the characters are overfamiliar to us. We know the endings of the plays only too well. As the extract from Peter Brook's *The Empty Space* on pages 194–5 showed, someone who does not know a play or a part will perform it in a different way to someone who has, perhaps, been in the production before. Directors often direct a Shakespeare play several times in their career and certain ideas are retained from production to production. To appreciate the boy players we should tear away these accepted traditions and try to look at the parts newly minted, to approach them as if we had no knowledge of them. Then we should see them as more simple, more dependent on the verse, than we do today.

Throughout this book we have seen that the boys were trained in the skills of the theatre. They had playwrights who wrote parts they could perform and gave them great verse and supple prose to speak, with metaphors to help them relate to the emotions they had to express. They were professionals in professional companies. If further confirmation that adolescent boys could play these parts convincingly is required, we have evidence from early in the last century. Laurence Olivier started his acting career with a talented amateur company belong to All Saints' Church, Margaret Street, London, where he had previously been a choirboy. Olivier played Katherine in *The Taming of the Shrew* in a company remarkable for the fact that boys acted with men, Olivier's Petruchio being the talented Father Geoffrey Heald. *The Shrew* was given in London and as the Birthday performance at the old theatre in Stratford-upon-Avon, just a month before Olivier's fifteenth birthday in 1922. Ellen Terry, who saw one of the London performances, commented that she had never seen Kate played better by a woman except Ada Rehan. Dame Sybil Thorndike, another member of the audience, said that Olivier was never overshadowed by his Petruchio, and that he was really 'wonderful, the best Shrew I ever saw – a bad-tempered little bitch . . .'. The actor Laurence Naismith, also in the cast, agrees, saying:

> Larry was born to act. He had the presence. What I remember about his Kate was his complete naturalness. . . . He was a very unattractive boy, lean and bony, with very skinny legs. And yet the moment he put

on those dresses his image and bearing changed completely. He really became a young girl.

[Cottrell, Laurence Olivier, p. 28]

Olivier was an actor of genius, but what he did – that is really become a young girl in his own mind and in the mind of his audience – is something, I submit, the boy players in Shakespeare's day could and did accomplish.

Punctuation of Ophelia's Speech, Hamlet, Act 3 scene i

'O, What a Noble Mind'

Quarto 1603, Quarto Facsimile, Oxford, 1965

Ofe. Great God of Heauen, what a quicke change is this?
The Courtier, Scholler, Souldier, all in him.
All dafht and fplinterd thence, O woe is me,
To a feene what I haue feene, fee what I fee. *Exit.*

Quarto 1604, San Marino, California, 1964

Oph. O what a noble mind is heere orethrowne!
The Courtiers, fouldiers, fschollers, eye, tongue, fword,
Th'expectation, and Rofe of the faire ftate,
The glaffe of fafhion, and the moulde of forme,
Th'obferu'd of all obferuers, quite quite downe,
And I of Ladies moft deiect and wretched,
That fuckt the honny of his mufickt vowes;
Now fee what noble and moft foueraigne reafon
Like fweet bells iangled out of time, and harfh
That vnmatcht forme, and ftature of blowne youth
Blafted with extacie, o woe is mee
T'haue feene, fee what I fee. *Exit.*

First Folio, 1623, Facsimile, 1923

OPHE. O what a Noble minde is heere o're-throwne?
The Courtiers, Soldiers, Schollers: Eye, tongue, fword
Th'expectanfie and Rofe of the faire State

The glaffe of Fashion, and the mould of Forme,
Th'obferv'd of all Obferuers, quite, quite downe.
Have I of ladies moft deiect and wretched,
That fuck'd the Honie of his Muficke vowes:
Now fee that Noble, and moft Soueraigne Reafon,
Like fweet Bels iangled out of tune, and harfh
That vnmatch'd Forme and Feature of blowne youth,
Blafted with extafie. Oh woe is me,
T'have feene what I haue feene: fee what I fee.

Cambridge Shakespeare, Cambridge, 1948

Ophelia. O, what a noble mind is here o'erthrown!
The courtier's, soldier's, scholar's, eye, tongue, sword,
Th' expectancy and rose of the fair state,
The glass of fashion, and the mould of form,
Th'observed of all observers, quite quite down,
And I of ladies most deject and wretched,
That sucked the honey of his music vows,
Now see that noble and most sovereign reason
Like sweet bells jangled, out of tune and harsh,
That unmatched form and feature of blown youth,
Blasted with ecstasy! O, woe is me!
T'have seen what I have seen, see what I see! (*she prays*)

The Pelican Shakespeare, Baltimore, 1957, revised 1960

Ophelia. O, what a noble mind is here o'erthrown!
The courtier's, soldier's, eye, tongue, sword,
Th' expectancy and rose of the fair state,
The glass of fashion and the mould of form,
Th'observed of all observers, quite, quite, down!
And I, of ladies most deject and wretched,
That sucked the honey of his music vows,
Now see that noble and most sovereign reason
Like sweet bells jangled, out of time and harsh,

That unmatched form and feature of blown youth
Blasted with ecstasy. O, woe is me
T'have seen what I have seen, see what I see!

Oxford Shakespeare, first published 1988, edition used 1991

OPHELIA
O what a noble mind is here o'erthrown!
The courtier's, soldier's, scholar's eye, tongue, sword,
Th'expectancy and rose of the fair state,
The glass of fashion and the mould of form,
Th'observed of all observers, quite, quite, down!
And I, of ladies most deject and wretched,
That sucked the honey of his music vows,
Now see that noble and most sovereign reason
Like sweet bells jangled, out of time and harsh,
That unmatched form and feature of blown youth
Blasted with ecstasy. O, woe is me
T'have seen what I have seen, see what I see!

Punctuated for Speaking

OPHELIA
* O what a noble mind is here o'erthrown *
The courtiers soldiers scholars eye tongue sword
Th'excpectancy and rose of the fair state *
The glass of fashion and the mould of form
Th'observed of all observers quite quite down *
And I of ladies most defect and wretched
That sucked the honey of his music vows *
Now see that noble and most sovereign reason
Like sweet bells jangled out of tune and harsh *
That unmatched form and feature of blown youth
Blasted with ecstasy * O woe is me
T'have seen what I have seen see what I see.

The Sumptuary Laws

1. Men's Apparel

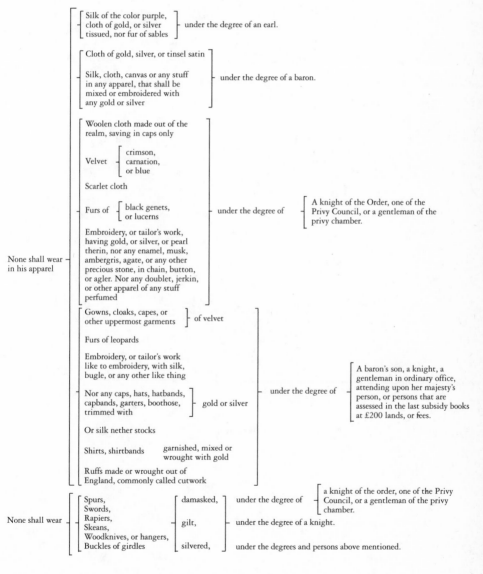

None shall wear in his apparel

- ⎡ Silk of the color purple, cloth of gold, or silver tissued, nor fur of sables ⎤ — under the degree of an earl.

- ⎡ Cloth of gold, silver, or tinsel satin

  Silk, cloth, canvas or any stuff in any apparel, that shall be mixed or embroidered with any gold or silver ⎤ — under the degree of a baron.

- ⎡ Woolen cloth made out of the realm, saving in caps only

  Velvet ⎡ crimson, carnation, or blue

  Scarlet cloth

  Furs of ⎡ black genets, or lucerns

  Embroidery, or tailor's work, having gold, or silver, or pearl therin, nor any enamel, musk, ambergris, agate, or any other precious stone, in chain, button, or agler. Nor any doublet, jerkin, or other apparel of any stuff perfumed ⎤ — under the degree of ⎡ A knight of the Order, one of the Privy Council, or a gentleman of the privy chamber.

- ⎡ Gowns, cloaks, capes, or other uppermost garments ⎤ — of velvet

  Furs of leopards

  Embroidery, or tailor's work like to embroidery, with silk, bugle, or any other like thing

  Nor any caps, hats, hatbands, capbands, garters, boothose, trimmed with ⎤ — gold or silver

  Or silk nether stocks

  Shirts, shirtbands — garnished, mixed or wrought with gold

  Ruffs made or wrought out of England, commonly called cutwork ⎤ — under the degree of ⎡ A baron's son, a knight, a gentleman in ordinary office, attending upon her majesty's person, or persons that are assessed in the last subsidy books at £200 lands, or fees.

None shall wear

- ⎡ Spurs, Swords, Rapiers, Skeans, Woodknives, or hangers, Buckles of girdles ⎤

  - ⎡ damasked, ⎤ — under the degree of ⎡ a knight of the order, one of the Privy Council, or a gentleman of the privy chamber.

  - gilt, — under the degree of a knight.

  - silvered, ⎤ — under the degrees and persons above mentioned.

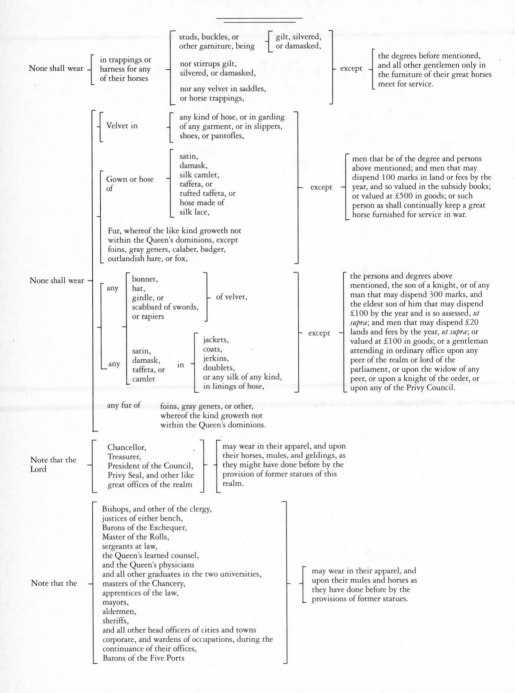

None shall wear — in trappings or harness for any of their horses

studs, buckles, or other garniture, being — gilt, silvered, or damasked,

nor stirrups gilt, silvered, or damasked,

nor any velvet in saddles, or horse trappings,

except — the degrees before mentioned, and all other gentlemen only in the furniture of their great horses meet for service.

Velvet in — any kind of hose, or in garding of any garment, or in slippers, shoes, or pantofles,

Gown or hose of — satin, damask, silk camlet, taffeta, or tufted taffeta, or hose made of silk lace,

Fur, whereof the like kind groweth not within the Queen's dominions, except foins, gray geners, calaber, badger, outlandish hare, or fox,

except — men that be of the degree and persons above mentioned; and men that may dispend 100 marks in land or fees by the year, and so valued in the subsidy books; or valued at £500 in goods; or such person as shall continually keep a great horse furnished for service in war.

None shall wear —

any — bonnet, hat, girdle, or scabbard of swords, or rapiers — of velvet,

any — satin, damask, taffeta, or camlet — in — jackets, coats, jerkins, doublets, or any silk of any kind, in linings of hose,

except — the persons and degrees above mentioned, the son of a knight, or of any man that may dispend 300 marks, and the eldest son of him that may dispend £100 by the year and is so assessed, *ut supra*; and men that may dispend £20 lands and fees by the year, *ut supra*; or valued at £100 in goods; or a gentleman attending in ordinary office upon any peer of the realm or lord of the parliament, or upon the widow of any peer, or upon a knight of the order, or upon any of the Privy Council.

any fur of — foins, gray genets, or other, whereof the kind groweth not within the Queen's dominions.

Note that the Lord — Chancellor, Treasurer, President of the Council, Privy Seal, and other like great offices of the realm — may wear in their apparel, and upon their horses, mules, and geldings, as they might have done before by the provision of former statues of this realm.

Note that the — Bishops, and other of the clergy, justices of either bench, Barons of the Exchequer, Master of the Rolls, sergeants at law, the Queen's learned counsel, and the Queen's physicians and all other graduates in the two universities, masters of the Chancery, apprentices of the law, mayors, aldermen, sheriffs, and all other head officers of cities and towns corporate, and wardens of occupations, during the continuance of their offices, Barons of the Five Ports — may wear in their apparel, and upon their mules and horses as they have done before by the provisions of former statues.

2. *Women's Apparel*

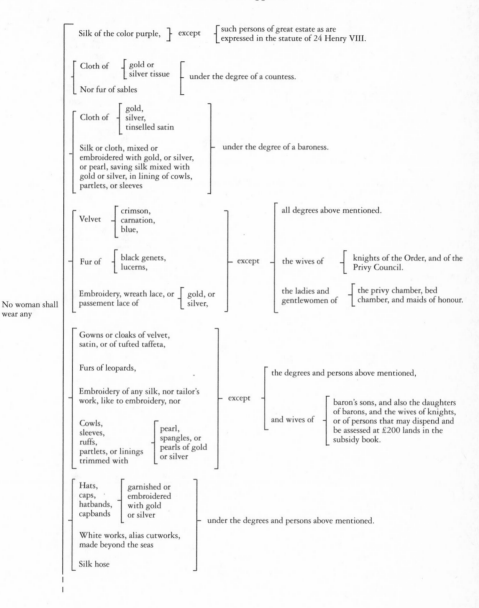

No woman shall wear any

Silk of the color purple, } except { such persons of great estate as are expressed in the statute of 24 Henry VIII.

[Cloth of { gold or silver tissue
Nor fur of sables] [under the degree of a countess.

[Cloth of { gold, silver, tinselled satin
Silk or cloth, mixed or embroidered with gold, or silver, or pearl, saving silk mixed with gold or silver, in lining of cowls, partlets, or sleeves] — under the degree of a baroness.

[Velvet { crimson, carnation, blue,
Fur of { black genets, lucerns,
Embroidery, wreath lace, or passement lace of { gold, or silver,] — except

all degrees above mentioned.

the wives of { knights of the Order, and of the Privy Council.

the ladies and gentlewomen of { the privy chamber, bed chamber, and maids of honour.

[Gowns or cloaks of velvet, satin, or of tufted taffeta,
Furs of leopards,
Embroidery of any silk, nor tailor's work, like to embroidery, nor
Cowls, sleeves, ruffs, partlets, or linings trimmed with { pearl, spangles, or pearls of gold or silver] — except

the degrees and persons above mentioned,

and wives of { baron's sons, and also the daughters of barons, and the wives of knights, or of persons that may dispend and be assessed at £200 lands in the subsidy book.

[Hats, caps, hatbands, capbands { garnished or embroidered with gold or silver
White works, alias cutworks, made beyond the seas
Silk hose] — under the degrees and persons above mentioned.

209

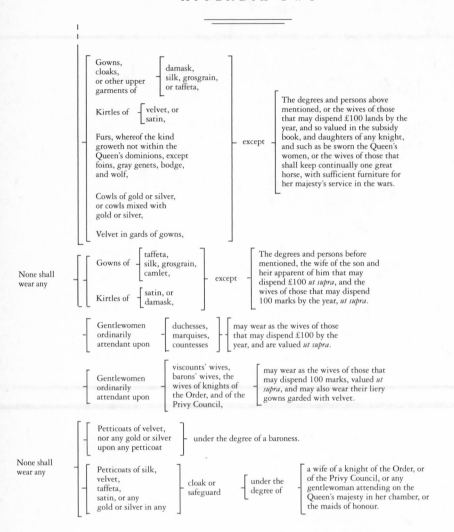

No person under the degrees above specified shall wear any gard or welt of silk upon any cloak or safeguard.

The modernised text is taken from Hughes and Larkin, Tudor Royal Proclamations, Proclamation 646 (1580), 2:458–61.

Bibliography

SUGGESTED FURTHER READING

Stanley Wells' *Shakespeare A Dramatic Life* gives an excellent commentary on the individual plays. Andrew Gurr's *Playgoing in Shakespeare's London* is the standard work on the buildings and the people who went to see the plays. John Barton's *Playing Shakespeare* reproduces his television master classes with RSC actors.

For Chapter One see particularly Gerald Eades Bentley, *The Profession of Player in Shakespeare's Time*; Muriel Bradbrook, *The Rise of the Common Player*; David Mann, *The Elizabethan Player*; Louis Wright, *Middle-Class Culture in Elizabethan England*.

For Chapter Two: Janet Arnold, *Queen Elizabeth's Wardrobe Unlock't*; Juliet Dusinberre, *Shakespeare and the Nature of Women*; Lisa Jardine, *Still Harping on Daughters*.

For Chapter Three: David Bevington, *Action is Eloquence: Shakespeare's Language of Gesture*; David Wulstan, *Tudor Music*.

For Chapter Four: George Wright, *Shakespeare's Metrical Art*; Tirzah Lowen, *Peter Hall Directs Antony and Cleopatra*.

For Chapters Seven and Eight: Reavley Gair, *The Children of St Paul's*; Michael Shapiro, *Children of the Revels*.

For Chapter Nine: Linda Woodbridge, *Women and the English Renaissance: Literature and the Nature of Womankind, 1540–1620*.

BIBLIOGRAPHY

GENERAL BIBLIOGRAPHY

Arnold, Janet, *Queen Elizabeth's Wardrobe Unlock't* (London, 1988)

Ashelford, Jane, *Dress in the Age of Elizabeth* (London, 1988)

Austern, Linda Phyllis, *Music in English Children's Drama of the Late Renaissance* (Indiana, 1992)

Baldwin, Thomas Whitfield, *The Organisation and Personnel of the Shakespearean Company* (Princeton, 1927)

Barber, C.L., *Shakespeare's Festive Comedy* (New Jersey, 1959)

Barker, Harley Granville, *Prefaces to Shakespeare*, Vol. VI (London, 1976)

Barton, John, *Playing Shakespeare* (London, 1984)

Bedingfeld, Henry, *Oxburgh Hall* (Norwich, 1987)

Belsey, Catherine, *The Subject of Tragedy – Identity and Difference in Renaissance Drama* (London and New York, 1985)

Bentley, Gerald Eades, *The Profession of Player in Shakespeare's Time* (Princeton, 1984)

Bentley, William, *Notes on the Musical Instruments figured in the Windows of the Beauchamp Chapel, St Mary's Warwick. Birmingham Archaeological Society's Transactions*, Vol. LIII (Birmingham, 1928)

Berry, Cicely, *The Actor and His Text* (London, 1987)

Bevington, David, *Action is Eloquence: Shakespeare's Language of Gesture* (Cambridge, Mass. and London, 1984)

Bornstein, Diane, *The Lady in the Tower* (London, 1983)

Bradbrook, Muriel, *Shakespeare and the Use of Disguise in Elizabethan Drama: Essays in Criticism: Vol. 2* (London, 1952)

——, *The Rise of the Common Player* (London, 1962; edition used, 1964)

Bray, Alan, *Homosexuality in Renaissance England* (London, 1982)

Brecht, Bertold, *Brecht on Theatre*, translated by Willett (New York and London 1957; edition used, 1964)

Briggs, Julia, *This Stage-Play World: English Literature and its background 1580–1625* (Oxford, 1983)

Broadbent, J.B., *Poetic Love* (London, 1964)

Brockbank, Philip, (ed) *Players of Shakespeare 1 – Essays in Shakespearean Performance by Twelve Players with the Royal Shakespeare Company* (Cambridge, 1985)

Brook, Peter, *The Empty Space* (London, 1968)

——, *The Shifting Point* (London, 1988)

Brooke, Iris, *English Costume in the Age of Elizabeth* (London, 1933)

Buxton, John, *Elizabethan Taste* (London and New York, 1966)

Castiglione, Baldesar, trans. George Bull, *The Book of the Courtier* (Harmondsworth, 1967)

Cecil, Lord David, *Hatfield House* (London, 1973)

Chatwin, Philip B., 'Some Notes on the Painted Windows of the Beauchamp Chapel, Warwick', *Birmingham Archaeological Society Transactions*, Vol. LIII (Birmingham, 1928), pp. 158–66

Colman, E.A.M., *The Dramatic Use of Bawdy in Shakespeare* (London, 1974)

Cook, Ann Jennalie, *Making a Match: Courtship in Shakespeare and his Society* (Princeton, NJ 1991)

Cook, Judith, *Women in Shakespeare* (London, 1980)

Cottrell, John, *Laurence Olivier* (revised edition, London, 1977)

Cox, Brian, *The Lear Diaries* (London, 1992)

Dash, Irene G., *Wooing, Wedding and Power: Women in Shakespeare's Plays* (New York, 1981)

Davies, W. Robertson, *Shakespeare's Boy Actors* (London, 1939)

Dawson, Anthony B., 'When Desdemona Meets Foucault: Discourse and the Performing Body' (Lecture given to the Shakespeare Institute, 1993)

Dollimore, Jonathan, *Radical Tragedy – Religion, Ideology and Power in the Drama of Shakespeare and his Contemporaries* (Brighton, 1984)

Dollimore J., and A. Sinfield (eds), *Political Shakespeare – New Essays in Cultural Materialism* (Manchester, 1985)

Dolmetsch, Mabel, *Dances of England and France 1450–1600* (London, 1949; edition used, 1959)

Donne, John, *Poems* (Oxford, 1944)

Drakakis (ed.), *Alternative Shakespeares* (London and New York, 1985)

Duncan-Jones, Katherine, *Sir Philip Sidney: Courtier Poet* (London, 1991)

Dusinberre, Juliet, *Shakespeare and the Nature of Women* (London, 1975; edition used, 1985)

Ferry, Anne, *The 'Inward' Language: Sonnets of Wyatt, Sidney, Shakespeare, Donne* (Chicago and London, 1983)

Fraser, Antonia, *The Six Wives of Henry VIII* (London, 1992)

Frye, Northrop, *On Shakespeare* (New Haven and London, 1986)

Gair, Reavley, *The Children of Paul's: the Story of a Theatre Company, 1553–1608* (Cambridge, 1982)

Greenblatt, Stephen, *Renaissance Self-Fashioning – from More to Shakespeare* (Chicago and London, 1980)

Gurr, Andrew, *The Shakespearean Stage 1574–1642* (Cambridge, 1982)

——, *Playgoing in Shakespeare's London* (Cambridge, 1987)

Hall, Peter, *Making an Exhibition of Myself* (London, 1993)

Haselkorn, A.M., and B.S. Travitsky (eds), *The Renaissance Englishwoman in Print* (Amherst, 1990)

Hazlitt, William, *Characters of Shakespeare's Plays* (London, 1817; edition used, 1921)

Hillebrand, Harold, *The Child Actors* (Urbana, 1926)

Howe, Elizabeth, *The First English Actresses* (Cambridge, 1992)

Hunter, G.K., *English Drama 1586–1642* (Oxford, 1997)

Jackson, R., and R. Smallwood (eds), *Players of Shakespeare 2 Further Essays in Shakespearean Performance by Players with the Royal Shakespeare Company* (first published Cambridge, 1988; edition used, 1990)

Jardine, Lisa, *Still Harping on Daughters – Women and Drama in the Age of Shakespeare* (Brighton and New Jersey, 1983)

Jonson, Ben, *The Alchemist* (London, 1992)

Kelly, F.M., *Shakespearean Costume for Stage and Screen* (London, 1938)

King, T.J., *Casting Shakespeare's Plays: London Actors and their Roles 1590–1642* (Cambridge, 1992)

Knott, Jan, *Shakespeare our Contemporary* (first published London, 1965; edition used, 1988)

Lancashire, Anne (ed.), *The Second Maiden's Tragedy* (Manchester and Baltimore, 1978)

Lever, J.W., *The Tragedy of State – A Study of Jacobean Drama* (first published London, 1971; edition used, 1987)

——, *The Elizabethan Love Sonnet* (London, 1956; edition used, 1966)

——, (ed.), *Sonnets of the English Renaissance* (London, 1974)

Long, John H., *Shakespeare's Use of Music: A Study of the Music and its Performance in the Original Production of Seven Comedies* (Gainesville, 1955)

——, *Shakespeare's Use of Music – The Final Comedies* (Gainesville, 1961)

Lowen, Tirzah, *Peter Hall Directs Antony and Cleopatra* (London, 1990)

Mann, David, *The Elizabethan Player* (London, 1991)

Maynard, Winifred, *Elizabethan Poetry and its Music* (Oxford, 1986)

Middleton, Thomas and William Rowley, *The Changeling* (London and New York, William 1990 edition used, 1991)

Middleton, Thomas and Thomas Dekker, *The Roaring Girl* (London, 1976)

Monk, Ray, *Ludwig Wittgenstein: The Duty of Genius* (London, 1990; edition used, 1991)

Morley, Thomas and R.A. Harman (eds), *A Plain and Easy Introduction to Practical Music* (London, 1952; edition used, 1966)

Naylor, Edward W., *Shakespeare and Music* (New York, 1965)

Norbrook, Davis, and H.R.Woudhuysen, *The Penguin Book of Renaissance Verse, 1509–1659* (London, 1992)

Olivier, Laurence, *Confessions of an Actor* (London, 1982)

Orgel, Stephen, 'Nobody's Perfect: Or Why Did the English Stage Take Boys for Women:' *The South Atlantic Quarterly*, 88...1 (Winter 1989)

——, 'Call me Ganymede: Shakespeare's Apprentices and the Representation of Women' (Lecture given to the Shakespeare Institute, Stratford-upon-Avon, 1990)

Partridge, Eric, *Shakespeare's Bawdy* (London, 1947; edition used, 1968)

Pitt, Angela, *Shakespeare's Women* (London and New Jersey, 1981)

Plato, *The Symposium*, translated by Hamilton (London, 1951; edition used, 1959)

Rose, Mary Beth, *The Expense of Spirit: Love and Sexuality in English Renaissance Drama* (Ithaca and London, 1988)

Rubinstein, Frankie, *A Dictionary of Shakespeare's Sexual Puns and their Significance* (London, 1984; edition used, 1989)

Rutter, Carol, *Clamorous Voices – Shakespeare's Women Today* (first published London, 1988; edition used, 1991)

Sartre, Jean-Paul, *The Psychology of Imagination* (London, 1972)

Schoenbaum, S., *William Shakespeare – A Compact Documentary Life* (revised edition, New York and Oxford, 1987)

Shakespeare, William, *The Complete Works* (Oxford, 1991)

Shapiro, Michael, *Children of the Revels – the Boy Companies of Shakespeare's Time and their Plays* (New York, 1977)

Shen, Lin, 'The Children of Paul's' (Phd Thesis, Mason Croft, The Shakespeare Institute, 1991)

Shirley, James, *Hyde Park* (London, 1987)

Sidney, Sir Philip, *Poems* (London, 1934)

Slater, Anne Pasternak, *Shakespeare the Director* (Brighton, 1982)

Spenser, Edmund, *The Poetical Works* (Oxford, 1912)

Stevens, John, *Music and Poetry in the Early Tudor Court* (London, 1961)

Strong, Roy, *Portraits of Elizabeth* (Oxford, 1963)

Sturgess, Keith (ed.), *Three Elizabethan Tragedies* (Harmondsworth, 1969; edition used, 1985)

Thompson, Craig R., *Schools in Tudor England, Essay in Life and Letters in Tudor and Stuart England*, eds Wright and La Mar (Ithaca, 1962)

Thomson, Peter, *Shakespeare's Theatre* (London and New York 1983; edition used, 1992)

Traub, Valerie, *Desire and Anxiety: Circulations of Sexuality in Shakespearian Drama* (London, 1992)

Vickers, Brian, *The Artistry of Shakespeare's Prose* (London, 1968)

Warren, Roger, *Staging Shakespeare's Last Plays* (Oxford, 1990)

Webster, John, *Three Plays* (London 1986)

Wells, S. (ed.), *The Cambridge Companion to Shakespeare Studies* (first published, Cambridge, 1986; edition used, 1991)

——, *Shakespeare: A Dramatic Life* (London, 1994)

Wiggins, Martin (ed.), *Four Jacobean Sex Tragedies* (Oxford, 1998)

Williams, John (ed.), *A Collection of Shorter Poems from Skelton to Jonson* (New York, 1963)

Winter, Carl, *Elizabethan Miniatures* (Harmondsworth, 1943)

Woodbridge, Linda, *Women and the English Renaissance: Literature and the Nature of Womankind, 1540–1620* (Brighton, 1984)

Worthen, William B., *The Idea of the Actor: Drama and the Ethics of Performance* (Princeton, NJ, 1984)

Wright, George T., *Shakespeare's Metrical Art* (Berkeley, LA and London, 1988)

Wright, Louis, *Middle-Class Culture in Elizabethan England* (first published, Carolina, 1935; edition used, Ithaca, NY, 1958)

Wright, L., and V. La Marr (eds), *Life and Letters in Tudor and Stuart England* (Ithaca, NY 1958; edition used, 1963)

Wulstan, David, *Tudor Music* (London, 1985)

Zimmerman, Susan, *Erotic Politics: Desire on the Renaissance Stage* (London and New York, 1992)

Index